ff

faber and faber

Moira Buffini

Gabriel

Winner of the LWT Award 1996

Soho Theatre Company...

...at the Soho Poly

In 1972 Verity Bargate and Fred Proud established the Soho Theatre Company at the 50 seat Soho Poly. The mission was to produce new plays and discover new playwrights and the Company was to become a pioneering force in British Theatre. Throughout the 70's and 80's the early work of such writers as Caryl Churchill, David Edgar, Hanif Kureishi, Tony Marchant, Sue Townsend and Timberlake Wertenbaker was premiered until the theatre – never an ideal performing space – was finally closed in 1990.

...at the Cockpit

'If there is going to be any theatre apart from musicals in twenty years time, the Soho Theatre Company will probably have been its seed bed.'
The Tatler

Under the new Artistic Direction of Abigail Morris, Soho Theatre Company relaunched in 1992 at the Cockpit Theatre. In three years there the Company presented more than 35 new plays and, in the words of the Ham and High created **'one of the leading centres for new writing in the country'**.

Plays premiered at the Cockpit included Karen Hope's *Ripped*; John Constable's *Tulip Futures*; Jonathan Lewis' *Our Boys*, Daniel Magee's *Paddywack* and Diane Samuels' *Kindertransport*.

...at 21 Dean Street

Soho Theatre Company will continue to produce elsewhere throughout the construction period. If you would like to be kept up to date, please call us on **0171 287 5060** to join our **free** mailing list.

In July 1996 Soho Theatre Company took possession of the spectacular premises that will become our new and permanent home – **21 Dean Street**. In successfully acquiring the £3.1 million freehold, we became the first arts organisation to purchase a property on the open market with National Lottery funding.

With the building secure, Soho Theatre Company are entering the second phase of the project – the conversion of the building into the **Soho Theatre and Writers' Centre**. Scheduled to open in 1999 it will include an intimate theatre space, comprehensive backstage and rehearsal facilities, a Writers' Centre to house our pioneering development work with new writers and a lively bar/cafe. Designed by award-winning architects Paxton Locher, the new building will become a unique theatre where you can see the first works of a new generation of writers, right in the heart of the West End.

But before we let the builders in, we wanted to give a sneak preview. Moira Buffini's **Gabriel** is part of **Site Specific**, a season of four new plays and a Writers' Showcase running until July 1997. We hope you enjoy the season and look forward to welcoming you back to 21 Dean Street in the future.

Soho Theatre Company – a Writers' Theatre

Soho Theatre Company is a writers' theatre. Not only are we committed as a matter of policy to the production of new plays exclusively, but the company actively encourages new and emerging writers through its training and development programme. Central to our philosophy is the belief that playwriting – like any other craft – must be practiced to develop. We provide:

A script service reporting on over 1500 scripts every year

A comprehensive writers' workshop programme

Rehearsed play readings

Script surgeries – *one to one dramaturgical support*

Writers' showcase productions

The Verity Bargate Award – *a biennial playwriting competition*

A bold commissioning policy

Send a play into our script reading service
At no cost to the writer, our readers' panel of theatre professionals will read, assess and advise on any play sent to us. Based on this assessment a decision will be made whether to consider the play further and how we might be able to help the writer develop their script.

The Workshop Programme
Writers showing promise may be invited to attend one of our various workshops. These range from skills workshops designed to heighten the participants' awareness of stagecraft, to those designed to examine in detail the writers' work-in-progress.

Writer's note

Gabriel was commissioned by
Paul Sirett in September 1995, and I
owe him a great deal of thanks for
his help and encouragement. I would
also like to thank Fiona, Nuala and
Susan Buffini, Sonia and Patricia
Gannon, St John Donald and
Rosie Cobb and Martin Biltcliffe, my
husband, all of whom have helped
and supported me through the
writing process.

Moira Buffini

With thanks to
Claire Blackburn
Sheila Buckland
Donna Gower
Vanessa Manship
Abigail Morris
The Royal Court

*First performed on 1 May 1997 at
Soho Theatre Company's new premises
at 21 Dean Street*

Soho Theatre Company presents

Gabriel by **Moira Buffini**

Cast
in order of appearance

Estelle Becquet	**Gemma Eglinton**
Lake	**Gillian Goodman**
Lily	**Jennifer Scott-Malden**
Von Pfunz	**Philip Fox**
Jeanne Becquet	**Lisa Harrow**
Gabriel	**Stephen Billington**

Director	Fiona Buffini
Designer	Julian McGowan
Lighting Designer	Jason Taylor
Assistant Director	Alison Newman
Sound equipment	Tetrus Sounds
German translations	Antje Menna
Costume Supervisor	Fionnuala Quinn
Casting	Marcia Gresham
Marketing and advertising	Hardsell 0171 403 4037
Press representation	Bridget Thornborrow Arts Publicity 0171 379 3797
Publicity photographs	Stuart Colwill
Production Manager	Julian Cree
DSM	Nicole Woodwood
ASM	Christopher Enticott
Set Construction	Steel the Scene
Box Office	First Call

Stephen Billington – *Gabriel*
Stephen trained at the Drama
Centre. Theatre work includes
The White Devil (Director Gale
Edwards); *Macbeth* (Director Tim
Albery) and *Troilus and Cressida*
(Director Ian Judge) all for RSC.
Television includes *The Man Who
Made Husbands Jealous*, Anglia
TV; *Out of the Blue*, BBC; *Rules of
Engagement*, YTV; *Space
Precinct*, Mentorn, and
The Buccaneers, BBC. Film work
includes Mel Gibson's *Braveheart*,
Balderstone Films.

Fiona Buffini – *Director*
*BA (Hons) Sussex University.
Postgraduate Directors' course at
Welsh College of Music and
Drama.* Theatre work includes
Jordan by Moira Buffini and
Anna Reynolds at The Gate; *Red*
by Anna Reynolds, UK Tour;
Othello and *Much Ado About
Nothing*, Bute Theatre, Cardiff;
Three and *Give Me Wings*,
Paradox Shuffle Dance
Company; Dostoevsky's
Underground Man and
Pirandello's *The Man with the
Flower in His Mouth* at St
Steven's Theatre, Cardiff; *The
Love of a Good Man* by Howard
Barker, and *Richard III*, Arts
Threshold; *Ecstasy* by Mike Leigh,
Latchmere Theatre; *Road* by Jim
Cartwright, The Faroe Islands.
Fiona has also worked with
Augusto Boal, Mike Alfreds and
Eugenio Barba.

Moira Buffini – *Writer*
Moira trained as an actor at The
Welsh College of Music and
Drama. She won a Time Out
Award for her performance in
Jordan, which she co-wrote with
Anna Reynolds. It won the
Writers' Guild Award for Best
Fringe play, 1992. Since then, she
has written *Blavatsky's Tower*;
Temp for Carlton TV's City Lights
series, and *Melissa Malone*, a
screenplay for BBC Wales. She is
currently working on *Silence*, a
new play for the National Theatre
Studio.

Gemma Eglinton – *Estelle*
Gemma is a pupil of the Jackie
Palmer Stage School in High
Wycombe. Theatre work includes
An Inspector Calls at the Aldwych
Theatre ; Alice in *Alice's
Adventures Underground* at the
Royal National Theatre. Television
work includes *One Foot in the
Grave; Next of Kin* and most
recently Helen in *Jane Eyre*, LWT.

Philip Fox – *Von Pfunz*
Philip trained at RADA. Theatre
work includes Dromio in *The
Comedy of Errors*, Regent's Park
(Director Ian Talbot); Flute in *The
Fairy Queen* (Director Adrian
Noble); Dicky Sainsbury in
Donkey's Years, Crucible, Sheffield
(Director Michael Rudman); *Mr A's
Amazing Maze Plays* and Foigard
in *The Beaux Stratagem* for Alan
Ayckbourn's company in
Scarborough. Recent television
includes Dr Hillman in *Bliss; Moll
Flanders; Degrees of Error;* Harry

the Swami in *The Brittas Empire* and Marvin Whipple in *Don't Tell Father*. Film work includes *Maurice* and *Solitaire for Two*. Recently read Lynne Truss' book, *With One Lousy Free Packet of Seed* for Radio 4.

Gillian Goodman – *Lake*
Theatre work includes Mrs Malaprop in *The Rivals,* Magnificent Theatre Company (Director Ben Crocker); Lady of Letters in *Talking Heads* and Big Mama in *Cat on a Hot Tin Roof,* both at Harrogate (Director Andrew Manley); *Comedy of Errors*, Nottingham (Director Paul Clayton); *Jane Eyre*, York Theatre Royal (Director John Adams); *When We are Married* and *Granny and the Gorilla* for West Yorkshire Playhouse (Directors John Adams and Michael Birch); *Pride and Prejudice*, Royal Exchange (Director James Maxwell); *Sisterly Feelings* and *The Old Order*, both for Leeds Playhouse (Directors, John North and John Harrison); *A Taste of Honey*, Leicester Phoenix (Director Val Baxter); *The Merry Wives of Windsor*, Derby Playhouse (Director David Milne); *Way Upstream*, Bolton Octagon (Director John Adams); *Balmoral*, Leeds Playhouse (Director John Harrison); *Forty Years On*, Harrogate (Director Ivor Benjamin); Mrs Warren in *Mrs Warren's Profession*, and *Uncle Vanya*, both for Harrogate (Director Andrew Manley); *Guys and Dolls* and Lady Bracknell in

The Importance of Being Earnest, The Forum, Manchester (Director Chris Honer); *A Little Hotel on the Side*, and *The Mayor of Casterbridge*, Cheltenham (Directors Martin Houghton and Ian Forrest). Television work includes *The Bill*, Thames TV; *Pigeon Summer*, Catalyst TV; *Waiting for God*, BBC; *Hard Cases*, Central; *First of the Summer Wine*, BBC; *The Rainbow*, BBC; *Snakes and Ladders*, YTV; *Booktower*, YTV, and *Double First*, BBC. Gillian has worked extensively for radio and her work includes Sandra and Mrs Walker in *The Archers,* George Elliot as Narrator in *Adam Bede* and Marthe in *Pillars of Society.*

Lisa Harrow – *Jeanne*
Theatre work includes extensive work for the RSC, including Olivia in *Twelfth Night*; Desdemona in *Othello*; Portia in *Merchant of Venice*; Anne Boleyn in *Henry VIII* and Dorcas in *A Winters Tale.* Other productions for them include *EARWIG, The Hollow Crown, Island of the Mighty, Major Barbara, Wild Oats* and *The Lower Depths.* Other work for the theatre includes Viola in *Twelfth Night*, Newcastle; Juliet in *Romeo and Juliet*, Coventry; *The Great Caper*, The Royal Court; Eliza in *Pygmailion,* Cambridge Theatre; *Wild Oats,* West End; *Man and Superman,* Triumph Apollo, Windsor and Playhouse Theatre; *Double Take,* Festival Theatre, Chichester

(Director Hugh Wooldridge);
Widower's House, Chelsea Centre
(Director Sharon Maughan);
The Eagle Has Two Heads, Lillian
Baylis Theatre (Director Susannah
York); *Dogspot*, Nuffield Theatre,
Sheffield (Director Patrick
Sandford); and *In Praise of Love*,
Leatherhead and West End
(Director Richard Olivier).
Television includes *Rivals of
Sherlock Holmes*, Thames; *The
Water Maiden*, BBC; *Churchill's
People*, BBC; *The Expert*, BBC;
The Look, Yorkshire; *Marya*, BBC;
Jekyll and Hyde, BBC; *The
Waterfall*, BBC; *Nancy Astor*, BBC;
Under Capricorn, South
Australian Film Corp; *Playing
Shakespeare*, LWT; *A Sense of
Guilt*, BBC; *Inspector Morse IV*,
Zenith Productions; *Poirot*, LWT;
Witchcraft, BBC; *The Strawberry
Tree*, Meridian; and *Kavannagh
QC*, Central. Film includes *The
Tempter; All Creatures Great and
Small; It Shouldn't Happen to a
Vet; Man from a Far Country;
Other Halves; Shaker Run; The
Final Conflict; The Last Days of
Chez Nous* (winner Best Actress
Australian Film Institute); *That
Eye in the Sky*. Her last film,
Sunday, won the 1997 Sundance
Festival Grand Jury Prize.

Julian McGowan – *Designer*
Julian trained at the Central
School of Art and Design. His
designs for theatre include *Don
Juan, The Lodger* and *Women
Laughing*, Royal Exchange,
Manchester; *The Possibilities* and
The LA Plays, The Almeida;

Making History (set only), Royal
National Theatre; *Heart Throb*,
The Bush; *Prin*, Lyric
Hammersmith and The West End;
Leonce and Lena, Crucible,
Sheffield; *The Rivals, Man and
Superman, Playboy of the
Western World* and *Hedda
Gabler*, Citizens, Glasgow;
Imagine Drowning and
Punchbag, Hampstead; *Tess of
the Durbevilles*, West Yorkshire
Playhouse; *The Changeling* (set
only) and *The Wives' Excuse*, RSC;
A Dolls House, Theatr Clwyd;
Torquato Tasso, Edinburgh
Festival; *American Bagpipes* and
The Treatment, The Royal Court;
Three Sisters, Break of Day and
The Steward of Christendom, The
Royal Court and Out of Joint; *Old
Times*, Theatr Clwyd and the
West End; *Caesar and Cleopatra,
Total Eclipse* and *A Tale of Two
Cities*, Greenwich Theatre. Opera
designs include *Cosi Fan Tutte*,
New Israeli Opera; *Eugene
Onegin*, Scottish Opera and *Siren
Song*, Almeida Opera Festival.
Most recent work includes *Simply
Disconnected*, Minerva,
Chichester; *Translations*, Abbey
Theatre, Dublin; *Shopping and
Fucking*, Ambassadors Theatre
and Out of Joint; *Hamlet*,
Greenwich Theatre and tour and
The Positive Hour, Hampstead
Theatre and Out of Joint.

Alison Newman – *Assistant Director*
Alison trained at Manchester Polytechnic School of Theatre. Acting jobs include *The Tempest,* Royal Exchange; *Electronic Dark Age,* Edinburgh Festival and *The Censor* by Anthony Neilson. Work as Assistant Director includes *Hoover Bag* by Anthony Neilson at the Young Vic Studio and *The Censor* by Anthony Neilson. Alison has also written several publications for BBC Childrens' Books.

Jennifer Scott-Malden – *Lily*
Jennifer trained at Bristol Old Vic Theatre School. Theatre work includes *The Merchant of Venice,* Sheffield Crucible (Director Deborah Paige); *White Unto Harvest,* The Red Room (Director Lisa Goldman); Nora in *A Doll's House,* Orchard Theatre Company (Director Bill Buffrey); Gwendolen in *The Importance of Being Earnest,* English Touring Theatre (Director Nick Wright); Estella in *Great Expectations,* Queens Theatre, Hornchurch (Director Tal Rubins); *Pericles,* National Theatre (Director Phyllida Lloyd); *Wild Things,* Salisbury Playhouse/Paines Plough tour (Director Deborah Paige). Film includes *Scandal,* Palace Pictures. Radio includes Hippolyta in *A Midsummer Night's Dream,* BBC Bristol, and *Gladiators,* Radio 4.

Jason Taylor – *Lighting Designer*
Theatre credits include *You Never Can Tell,* West Yorkshire Playhouse; *The Seagull,* Orange Tree, Richmond; *Romeo and Juliet,* Scarborough; *Tulip Futures,* Soho Theatre Company; *The Glass Menagerie, The Woman Who Cooked Her Husband, Burn This* and *The Dresser,* Theatre Royal, Plymouth; *Misery, For Services Rendered* and *Forty Years On,* Scarborough; *A View From The Bridge,* York, Theatre Royal; *Office Suite,* West Yorkshire Playhouse; *Hay Fever,* Crucible, Sheffield; six seasons at the Open Air Theatre, Regents Park, including *A Midsummer Night's Dream, Hamlet, The Card, Richard III* and *The Music Man; And Then There Were None,* Duke of York's; *Rosencrantz and Guildenstern are Dead,* Piccadilly; *Kindertransport,* Vaudeville. National tours include *The Hobbit; Feed; Fallen Angels; Dancing at Lughnasa.* International work includes *Sweet Sorrow,* Los Angeles; *The Taming of the Shrew,* Middle East tour; *Blood Brothers,* New Zealand/Australia tour. Other work includes interior lighting design for *The Emaginator* at the Trocadero, London; Soho Theatre Company consultancy.

Gabriel

Everything possible to be believed
is an image of the truth

William Blake

faber and faber
LONDON · BOSTON

First published in 1997
by Faber and Faber Limited
3 Queen Square London WC1N 3AU

Typeset by Country Setting, Woodchurch, Kent TN26 3TB
Printed in England by Intype London Ltd

A CIP record for this book
is available from the British Library

ISBN 0–571–19327–7

2 4 6 8 10 9 7 5 3 1

In memory of John Buffini
and Antony Rose

Characters

Jeanne Becquet A collaborator
Estelle Her daughter, aged ten
Lily Her daughter-in-law
Lake A housekeeper
Von Pfunz A Nazi
Gabriel A lost man

Setting

An old farmhouse on the island of Guernsey.
February 1943. Hitler's occupying forces have
been on the island for two and a half years.

Scene One

A winter evening. The crumbling kitchen of a very old farmhouse: stone floors, an old stove. The table is piled up with boxes of groceries and crates of spirits. All is in darkness. Estelle, a child of ten, is lit by a single candle. She is drawing a chalk square around a flagstone. When it's finished, she makes some strange gestures with her hands. She puts her ear to the ground in the middle of the square, and listens.

Estelle   Don't let them come any nearer. Keep them away,
please keep them away . . .
I send my wish crashing through the rocks
that everything'll fall on them,
in the sky that their planes will crash in flames,
that the sea will roar with storms
and I say drown them all; destroy them all,
fling them to pieces for taking our house –
and let my brother come like a bright angel
to save me. Save me.

Lake, a housekeeper, enters carrying a lamp.

Lake   What are you doing?

Estelle   Nothing.

Lake   Well get up then. (*Puts the lamp on the table.*) And blow that candle out. I shouldn't think we'll get power back 'til morning now.

Estelle   I'm afraid I can't move just yet Mrs Lake.

Lake   Why not?

Estelle   I'm involved in something.

Lake   You were going to help me with these orders.

Estelle   Sorry.

Lake   Well . . . suit yourself. (*Sorting through boxes of groceries.*) Everything in at once and nowhere to blasted put it . . .

> *Lake starts to make up packages of goods tied with newspaper and string.*

Estelle   I'm listening to the men.

Lake   What?

Estelle   The men underneath.

Lake   Rubbish. They're miles away those tunnels; not even close.

Estelle   They're going to come right under.

Lake   Since when?

Estelle   I can hear the machines.

Lake   Course you can't.

Estelle   They're building a labyrinth, a huge labyrinth for the Krauts.

Lake   Not under here, they're not. We're too near the sea; they'd flood. And look, it's past nine o' clock. Even if they were down there, they'd have gone home to the camp for their tea, wouldn't they?

Estelle   They don't have any tea. They have a lump of bread – that big – a lump of mouldy bread.

Lake   How do you know?

Estelle   Everybody knows.

Lake   You ever gone in that camp and watched them eat?

Estelle   Course not.

Lake   Well then. Come and help me with these orders.

Estelle   I can't.

Lake   Why not?

Estelle   I'm in an enchantment.

Lake   Well, that's marvellous. (*As she fills an order.*) Shultz . . . Spam, a sugar . . . It's dwarves you can hear down there, working in their gold mine.

Estelle   Are you scared of them, Mrs Lake?

Lake   Those men? Course not.

Estelle   I am.

Lake   Why?

Estelle   They got faces like ghosts.

Lake   Well don't think about them. I'm sure I never do.

Estelle   I saw one in the lane when it was getting dark, all pale and bony. You never see them by themselves but this one was alone. He said something in foreign.

Lake   Nonsense.

Estelle   I had a sandwich in my pocket so I threw it at him and ran away. I looked over my shoulder and he was on his knees in front of it with his mouth open, horrible in the dark like a big O.

Lake   They got no business talking to you. Tinkers and sodomites from all o' Europe.

Estelle   D'you know what he was wearing under his jacket?

Lake   What?

Estelle A coal sack. They work in blackness down there, I imagine it at nights – miles of broken rocks and water dripping on their heads. I can hear them shouting in my dreams all foreign through the earth and when they collapse or die, the Krauts just shove them in the concrete. They bury them in the walls – did you know that?

Lake Rubbish.

Estelle If you climb up the barn you can see their camp –

Lake (*firmly*) No you can't. Get off the floor.

Estelle I don't want to.

Lake Why not?

Estelle Well. (*Suddenly smiling.*) I made something.

Lake What?

Estelle A square of power.

Lake Where?

Estelle I'm lying in it aren't I?

Lake Don't make me laugh.

Estelle Whoever's in it shall be compelled to take their clothes off and dance, nude.

Lake (*amused*) You little devil. Come on then.

Estelle What?

Lake Strip off; let's see you dancing.

Estelle I don't have to; I made it didn't I?

Lake (*laughing*) Square of power? You clown . . .

Estelle What?

Lake   A square of power don't mean a thing!

Estelle   It does.

Lake   Come on, out the way then and see if I strip off.

Estelle   Well you won't, will you? You know about it so you can defend yourself.

Lake   A *circle* is power, not a square; a circle.

Estelle   I don't want a circle.

Lake   (*laughs*) Square o' power . . .

Estelle   Stop laughing at me!

Lake   All the power in that's just goin' to seep out the corners.

Estelle   (*disappointed*) Is it? . . .

Lake   Course it is.

Estelle gets up and flops into a big leather chair, deeply upset. She curls up.

Lake   Schulë: one Spam, one coffee . . .

Estelle   (*close to tears*) I hate this house.

Lake   Oh sweetheart . . .

Estelle   I want The Hermitage back. What would Myles say if he knew there were Krauts living there?

Lake   Well now, –

Estelle   What if he knew you were selling them food? What if he knew that Mummy went out with that Captain?

Lake   Myles isn't here. He doesn't know what it's like – and if he was here he'd be doing same as us: coping. Anyway, your Mother doesn't go out with anyone – where did you hear that?

Estelle   I'm not stupid.

Lake   She was *friendly* with Captain Reicher but she never went out with him. And he's gone now, hasn't he? (*Pause.*) I know we've lost the big house but we're a lot better off than some: we got *officers* staying up there, not scum. Besides, this is a good little place; nothing wrong with it.

Estelle   It hasn't even got a bloody toilet.

Lake   Watch your mouth. Why don't you rub that mess out?

Estelle   It's not a mess, it's a square of power.

Lake   Fine.

The door opens. Lily enters, breathless, distressed. The chair hides Estelle from her.

Lily   Lake – I need you.

Lake   I'm busy.

Lily   There's a man down by the beach. I almost rode right over him. I can't get him on my bike.

Lake   What are you talking about?

Lily   He's unconscious. I need you to help me prop him up. Come on.

Lake   You must be joking.

Lily   Lake, he's dying and I need you to help me!

Lake   Who is he?

Lily   I don't know.

Lake   Well what's he wearing?

Lily   Nothing. It looks as though he's been in the sea. I think he must've crawled up the beach.

Lake   The beach is a minefield down there . . .

Lily   I know. We can't let him die. Can you imagine, for him to survive the minefield and then die because he's cold? . . . I put my coat round him but it's not enough. Come on.

Lake   You expect me to go with you just like that?

Lily   (*shocked*) Yes . . .

Lake   He's one of them foreigners, isn't he, from the camp?

Lily   He's dying.

Lake   Well I'm sorry, but I think you should leave well alone.

Lily   Lake!

Lake   I know it sounds hard, but you can't go around helping those people; you know you can't. He'll be some Pole or something, all eaten up with disease.

Lily   I don't believe it!

Lake   I'm sorry for the man, truly I am, but he's probably dead by now anyway and he shouldn't be your trouble.

Lily   I'm not leaving him.

Lake   Then go up The Hermitage and get the Krauts to help.

   Lily is speechless.

Estelle   I'll come.

Lily   (*noticing her for the first time*) You're supposed to be in bed.

Estelle   I'll get my coat.

Lake   You will not.

Estelle   Wait.

Estelle runs out of the kitchen. Lily calls after her.

Lily   Bring something to put round him!

Lake   I know what you think of me.

Lily   Do you?

Lake   But anyone in their right mind would do the same. You know the penalty for helping those men; signs are up everywhere.

Lily   I know.

Lake   One word: Death. They don't even tell you how. Woman from Câstel just complained, *complained* about screaming she heard in the camp and they tortured her.

Lily   No they didn't.

Lake   And those people who had one hiding in their house; sent away to camps in Europe, the whole family! . . . And when you got this naked corpse, what are you going to do with it? Cause you can't bring it here.

Lily   Course I can.

Lake   It's not your house.

Lily   It's not yours either! . . . (*More calmly.*) I *can't* leave him, Lake. I'd have nightmares.

Estelle returns, warmly dressed, carrying a blanket and an old coat.

Estelle   I'm ready, come on.

Lily   Besides, there isn't a mark on him. He's not from the camp.

Lake   A deserting Kraut then.

Lily   He might be English.

Lake   A suicide.

Estelle   Let's go.

Lily   What if he's English? That plane that came down over the bay this morning. What if it's him? Would you condemn him, Lake? A pilot like Myles?

Lily and Estelle leave. Lake is livid. She quietly fumes.

Lake   How dare you. Taking the child out. I'm not a coward, you bloody *cockney*. Madness. You're the coward, girl; you're scared o' the bloody pigs, scared to pluck the fowl. After the war he'll come home and sling you out. You don't even know him, you –

Suddenly the overhead lights come on. Lake starts with shock and turns to the light switch, as if someone has switched it on. Her groundless fear makes her even more angry.

Lake   NOW WHAT? Just to torment us . . . power back on when everyone's off to bed . . .

A car pulls up outside. Lake panics. She quickly begins to clear away the kitchen table, shoving food indiscriminately into crates and boxes. She extinguishes the lamp.

Lake   Oh no. Don't bring him in. Don't bring him in. You can't bring him in.

There's quite a lot of groceries remaining on the table, when Von Pfunz enters, short and formal, holding the door open for Jeanne. Jeanne, elegant and aloof, sweeps past him.

Jeanne   Hello Margaret, this is Major Von Pfunz . . .

Von Pfunz   Hallo good evening!

Jeanne stands in the chalk square as she speaks, and takes off her hat, coat and gloves. She holds them out for Lake.

Jeanne   He's new to the Channel Islands, so we must do our very best to make him feel welcome. He's taken over from our dear Captain Reicher.

Von Pfunz   Hallo, yes . . .

Jeanne   And he doesn't speak any English. He's a buffoon.

Lake nods at Von Pfunz. Von Pfunz grins back.

Jeanne   You see how cosy we've made things, Major? You wouldn't think we'd only been here a week. House; nice?

Von Pfunz   Very nice . . .

Von Pfunz is peering at one of Lake's boxes. Lake eyes him nervously.

Jeanne   We've managed to squeeze in more comfortably than we thought – although the bathroom facilities are proving quite a rural adventure. Ein Cognac?

Von Pfunz   Ja, ja, Cognac, very nice.

Jeanne approaches Lake on her way to get the drinks. Quietly:

Jeanne   Why can't you be more careful? A fool could tell what you've been doing.

Lake   I didn't know you were going to bring him back.

Jeanne   He insisted, you bloody stupid woman.

Lake   You have to get rid of him.

Jeanne   I want to find out where they've sent Reicher.

Lake   Not tonight. The cockney's gone running –

Jeanne   Anyway half his men buy from us; what's he going to do?

Von Pfunz   (*reading off a tin, smiling for approval*) Sardines in brine.

Jeanne   Mrs Lake has been collecting tirelessly for the church bazaar. (*To Lake.*) You see? He's an imbecile; what's the problem?

Lake   Get rid of him.

Jeanne   No.

Lake   I mean it.

Jeanne   Put Estelle to bed would you, Margaret? (*Turning to Von Pfunz with a drink.*) I hope your officers are appreciating The Hermitage, Major. Thanks for letting us take our bric-a-brac before you kicked us out. Here, Cognac. It's Captain Reicher's but I'm sure he won't mind. He's gone for good, hasn't he?

Von Pfunz   Thank you very much.

Jeanne   Still here, Mrs Lake?

Lake leaves.

Jeanne   Are the ghosts at The Hermitage bothering you at all? I do hope so. We're one of the oldest families on the island, so there's plenty of them. Lascalles is my maiden name and we go right back to the tenth century. My ancestors invaded Britain with William the Conqueror.

Von Pfunz giggles. It has started to rain.

Jeanne   What about yours? Tyrolean goat herds, perhaps. Did you wear leather shorts as a child? A nightmare for your mother when you wet them. Light me a ciggie, would you? Ein cigaretten bitte Von Major.

Von Pfunz   Ah! Ja, ja. Ciggie . . .

Von Pfunz lights cigarettes for himself and Jeanne, in a Hollywood kind of way.

Jeanne   (*unimpressed*) Thanks. So suave. Really, I'm powerless in your sway. Are you married? Do you cheat on your wife with prostitutes? Is she ugly too? My husband was ugly; there's no shame in it. He's been dead for five years now and I don't miss him at all . . . I married a pig. Well, of course I had to. I was pregnant with another man's child. My son's twenty-six now, so handsome it hurts you to look. He flies a plane for the RAF and he's going to die in the war, I know it. There's an ashtray over there. Ashtray. For flicken ashen. Can you fetch it?

Von Pfunz   Ah . . . ashenbecher! Ashtray. Ash Tray . . .

Von Pfunz eagerly fetches an ashtray.

Jeanne   Goodness, what rain! My son's name is Myles. Shall I tell you a secret? I have nothing to fear from you, have I? I *love* him . . . (*Pause.*) He left me three years ago and came back just before the war, married. Exactly the kind of girl he knew I'd hate; a little cockney madam and a Jew, to boot.

Von Pfunz chokes. Jeanne watches, unsympathetic.

Jeanne   Well, I must say it's been a very pleasant evening, Major. Very Nice Evening.

Von Pfunz   (*still coughing*) Ja. Schön. Very nice!

Jeanne   I enjoyed watching that piece of veal you had, stuck to your lip. Mmm. Nice Food.

Von Pfunz   Very nice food, ja.

Jeanne   I'd do anything for a good meal, you know. I'm so sick of the taste of Spam I'd probably even . . . Well;

these are hard times, aren't they? Of course, you're a
powerfully attractive man; one rarely encounters such an
erotic charge. I don't want to be personal, but is the rest
of you as shiny as your face? How do you keep up that
lustrous gloss? God, I wonder if I could bear it . . . No.
I'd have to be drunk or insane. Do tell me about your
wonderful name, Major; it sounds like flatulence. Where
does it come from? Von Pfunz – your name?

Von Pfunz   Ah! Twenty-nine October.

Jeanne   Well, I can see we're going to be firm friends!
Where did they send Captain Reicher? He's not coming
back, is he?

Von Pfunz   Cap-tain Reicher? (*He giggles.*) Ja!

Jeanne   Yes, hilarious isn't it? Did they send him to
Russia? . . . We were lovers but I'm sure you know that.
I'm sure you think you've come to take his place.
Fantastic. Lucky old me . . .

Von Pfunz   Fan*tas*tic!

Jeanne   Cheers.

They clink glasses.

Von Pfunz   Roll me over in the clover.

Jeanne   Oh dear.

Von Pfunz   Down the hatch.

*Von Pfunz drains his glass. Jeanne takes it from him
and refills it as she speaks.*

Jeanne   Hitler's done a lot for your country, hasn't he?
A lot of people here think so; you'd be surprised. That's
a splendid uniform, much smarter than ours. There's a lot
of people here who like the Krauts you know, especially
women, women who'll be sorry if you leave. Guernseymen

can be pigs you see, real *pigs*, and you're a very handsome
race. Some of you anyway. And some of you look like
goblins.

Von Pfunz   (*taking the brandy*) Nice thank you.

Jeanne   Most of us can differentiate between Germans
and Nazis you see. Germans are fairly acceptable in a dull,
teutonic kind of way, but you're a Nazi, I can tell. Reicher
talked a lot about Nazis. In general, he said there are
three kinds: The Fanatic, quite mad and therefore worthy
of serious respect; The Sycophant, who would follow
orders to shoot his own mother – and The Intellectual;
bright enough to know what's going on and brutal enough
not to care. Which kind are you?

Von Pfunz   (*in perfect English*) Oh, I must be the fourth
kind Mrs Becquet.

Jeanne   (*takes a sip of her drink*) I see. And what kind is
that?

Von Pfunz   He sits on a pale horse and his name is death.
So to speak. (*He bursts into peals of giggles.*) I've been
wonderfully entertained this evening. You're very
charming.

Jeanne   (*pause*) Thank you.

Von Pfunz   Is it true you slept with Reicher? – I didn't
know. I'm so sorry about my poor manners and my
unfortunate name. Von Pfunz. It comes from a small town
north of Munich.

Jeanne   How nice.

Von Pfunz   My father and mother ran a school for the
children of the rich. Not much time for herding goats.
They were very cultured and were kind enough not to
dress me in leather clothes. I never had a wife. Just never

met the right woman and if I did I would be loyal to her until death devoured me. There. I think I have answered all of your questions and now you can answer mine. When you said you'd do anything for a good meal, what did you mean?

Jeanne Well . . . nothing.

Von Pfunz What did you mean by my lustrous gloss?

Jeanne I didn't mean anything . . .

Von Pfunz You said you'd have to be drunk, or insane. To do what, exactly?

Jeanne I'm sorry, I don't remember saying that.

Von Pfunz unbuttons his jacket.

Von Pfunz Please be honest; I love the truth. I have erotic charge for you. You make a joke but this joke hides often what is true. You want to touch me; that is what you meant.

Jeanne I suppose it's too late for an apology?

Von Pfunz Don't demean yourself, Mrs Becquet. I'm not asking you to apologise.

Von Pfunz undoes his trousers. He takes Jeanne's drink from her. He sips it. He returns it. Jeanne puts out her hand to touch him. She withdraws it.

Jeanne I rather think I'm going to need my polish and a cloth.

Von Pfunz turns away furious and embarrassed. He does his trousers up. He turns back to Jeanne and lifts his hand to straighten his hair. Jeanne flinches in fear, as if about to be hit. Von Pfunz is genuinely surprised.

Von Pfunz Did you expect me to hit you?

Jeanne No.

Von Pfunz I think you did. You must believe in your heart that you deserved it.

Jeanne No.

Von Pfunz Force of habit then. Your husband was a violent man.

Jeanne No.

Von Pfunz But he was a pig?

Jeanne Your English is very good, Major.

Von Pfunz No really; I don't speak a word.

Jeanne Why did you stop me talking? I would've told you everything eventually.

Von Pfunz Was there any more to tell?

Jeanne Perhaps you were trying to protect me from myself.

Von Pfunz I was becoming bored.

Jeanne That's always a danger when you don't understand the language.

Von Pfunz I'm not surprised that Reicher was so taken with you; you must have had him in the palm of your hand. Did you know what his job was?

Jeanne I had an idea.

Von Pfunz It is to be my job too. Did he ever talk about it?

Jeanne Of course not.

Von Pfunz Did you ever ask him?

Jeanne I wasn't interested.

Von Pfunz Everyone is interested, Mrs Becquet. People do a good job at pretending the camps don't exist, but in reality, they want to know all about them. Have you ever been in a labour camp?

Jeanne No.

Von Pfunz All of life is there . . . Humanity in all its extremes. I've gained a deep, almost religious understanding of humanity from what I have seen in our camps. My job is to liaise, you see, between the work organisation and the military. The camps here are small and dull but in many ways I was glad to get the posting. It's certainly warmer than Poland.

Jeanne Yes.

Von Pfunz And so lovely. As I sailed past all the little islands, I thought it tragic that Homer lived too far south to sing their praises. Really, this place is a haven. Pretty gardens, antique churches – all the poet needs for inspiration. Do you think I will fit in?

Jeanne I'm afraid not.

Von Pfunz Why?

Jeanne I don't expect you fit in anywhere, do you?

Von Pfunz (*giggling, but shocked*) Oh dear! You really are the most insulting woman I've ever met!

Jeanne Forgive me.

Von Pfunz No, it's so refreshing . . . Do you tell a lot of lies Mrs Becquet?

Jeanne I generally lie all the time.

Von Pfunz But you tell the truth to me. Fan*tas*tic . . . (*Pause.*) How many people know that you married because you were pregnant with another man's child?

Jeanne   One.

Von Pfunz   Your husband never knew?

Jeanne   And never will.

Von Pfunz   And your . . . *liaison* with your son?

Jeanne   What?

Von Pfunz   That was your secret, wasn't it?

Jeanne   I said I loved him.

Von Pfunz   But we both know what you meant.

Jeanne   I hope I'm not being insulting again, Major, but you wouldn't know what I meant in a million years.

Von Pfunz   What happened to his wife, the Jew?

Jeanne   When the invasion looked imminent, she fled. Sailed off to England on a boat packed with cowards and I haven't seen her since. We were never close.

Von Pfunz   (*pause*) How long have you been trading on the black market?

Jeanne   Since the beginning of the war. Are you going to arrest me?

Von Pfunz   No.

Jeanne   Then perhaps we could drop the subject.

Von Pfunz   You're not a patriot, are you?

Jeanne   Of course I am. But I'm a pragmatist. My husband died heavily in debt. I've done only what was necessary to keep my house.

Von Pfunz   And now you've lost it to the Reich.

Jeanne   To you, yes.

Von Pfunz   Do you make a great deal of money?

Jeanne   That's really none of your business.

Von Pfunz   I could make it my business.

Jeanne   Then arrest me.

Von Pfunz   Not yet.

Jeanne   Why not?

Von Pfunz   I'm hoping we may become . . . well. I'd like to be – . (*He sighs.*) I have seen terrible things in this war. I have been ill with it. Ill in my soul . . .

Jeanne   (*coldly*) Oh dear.

Von Pfunz   (*smiles*) You are so *rude*, so completely dismissive . . . It's a long time since I met someone so . . . forthright and true. I'm hoping, perhaps we could –

Jeanne   Do I have any choice?

Von Pfunz   There's always an element of choice in human affairs. When someone tells you they have no choice they're invariably lying. They've merely assessed their position and gone for the line of least resistance; the option which will cause them least trouble. It's a local virtue apparently, amongst the brave Britishers of Guernsey . . . (*Approaching Jeanne, who is now in the chalk square.*)

> I'd like to look at you
> As you are, naked in the light
> Jeanne Lascalles.

Jeanne   Is that an order?

Von Pfunz   It's a poem.

> You are the one
> Who sees me as I am, and laughs
> Jeanne Lascalles.

Jeanne turns her back on Von Pfunz.

Von Pfunz   Do you dislike poetry?

Jeanne   Bad poetry, yes.

Von Pfunz   Of course; with such a fine poetic tradition, who could blame you? As a young man in Munich I spent many a happy evening curled up by the fireside with my Treasury of English Verse. So many fine men . . . so much delicate misery. I have always felt a kindred spirit. But you see,

> Blasted with sighs and surrounded by tears,
> Hither I come to seek the spring
> And at mine eyes and at mine ears
> Receive such balms as else cure everything.

Jeanne   Major.

Von Pfunz   (*touching Jeanne's shoulder*)

> But O, self traitor I do bring
> The spider love, which transubstantiates all
> And can convert manna to gall
> And that this place may thoroughly be thought
> True Paradise, I have the serpent brought.

Von Pfunz undoes the zip on Jeanne's dress. He slowly touches her skin. She suddenly turns round and looks at him with contempt. She pulls her dress off and throws it to the floor. She throws her shoes off. She lifts her arms to undo her bra.

Von Pfunz   (*shocked, hurt*) Stop!

Jeanne stops.

Von Pfunz   I see you are a prostitute.

Pause. The door opens and Estelle rushes in, soaked to the skin. She looks at them, aghast. Jeanne, leaving the chalk square, fumbles into her dress.

Jeanne   Estelle.

Von Pfunz   (*buffoon-like*) Hallo good evening!

Jeanne   Estelle . . .

Estelle leaves, slamming the door.

Jeanne   Estelle!

Jeanne opens the door and shouts into the darkness.

Jeanne   Estelle! . . .

Jeanne closes the door. She does up her dress, looking at the floor, consumed with shame and rage. Von Pfunz buttons his jacket.

Von Pfunz   I hope we haven't shocked the little lady . . .

Jeanne   Of course we have!

Von Pfunz   I thought she might be used to seeing her mother in various stages of undress with German officers.

Jeanne   GET OUT!!

Von Pfunz   Well, I'd love to stay and question her as to why she's outside, two hours after curfew, but some other day. My bedroom at the Hermitage is the one with panelled walls and a fine view of the sea. Was that yours? (*Pause.*) No. It doesn't seem like a womanly room. Perhaps it was your son's? . . .

Jeanne   It belonged to my late husband. I hope he haunts you.

Von Pfunz   Does he haunt you?

There is a knock at the door and Lily enters, soaking wet from the rain. She glances nervously at Von Pfunz.

Lily   We wanted to apologise for being out after curfew. There was a sick cow in the top field and I asked Estelle to come with me, to hold the torch. I'm sure we should have left it till the morning . . .

Jeanne   Get Estelle and go to your room.

Von Pfunz   (*buffoon-like*) Jeanne, please you introduce me?

Jeanne   Lilian, this is Major Von Pfunz. Major Von Pfunz, Lilian Becquet.

Von Pfunz   Hallo . . . Sister of Jeanne?

Jeanne   Yes –

Lily   No, I'm her daughter-in-law.

Von Pfunz   (*removing his hand*) Ah! . . . son's wife, son Myles; flies a plane?

Lily   That's right.

Von Pfunz   Very nice . . . Is cow better?

Lily   It's fine.

Von Pfunz   I have a look? I know many sick cow facts.

Lily   No, really – if it gets any worse, I can fetch the vet.

Von Pfunz   (*pointing to himself*) Better than vet!

Lily   Thanks, but Estelle and I got awfully wet in the rain. We rather want to dry off and go to bed now.

Von Pfunz   Well! Rather want very nice, dry off yes. Good evening. (*To Jeanne, kissing her hand.*) Enchanted. You are an oracle of truth.

   Von Pfunz leaves.

Jeanne   There are no cows on this farm, Lilian.

Lily   I meant to say pig . . . A sick pig.

Jeanne He'll find out.

Lily I meant to say pig and cow just popped out before I could –

Jeanne Until you learn to lie properly, you shouldn't try it! Where's Estelle?

Lily She's in the barn.

Jeanne What the hell is she doing outside at this time of night?

Lily Mrs Becquet, there's a sick man outside and I'm going to have to bring him in.

Jeanne What?

Lily I thought Lake would've told you.

Jeanne She told me nothing. What are you talking about? What sick man?

Lily I found him . . . on the beach. He's freezing to death and I need to bring him in.

Jeanne Who is he?

Lily I don't know; he hasn't spoken. He's unconscious.

Jeanne Well what's he wearing?

Lily Nothing . . .

Jeanne Nothing? He's naked and half dead and you're telling me he's on my doorstep? How *dare* you do this . . .

Lily Please, he's dying . . .

Jeanne Not in my house, Lilian!

Lily Please! Estelle's with him in the barn, covering him with straw to keep him warm but he'll die soon, if we don't help him!

Jeanne   You've left my daughter alone in the barn with a naked man?

Lily   I put a coat round him!

Jeanne   Good God!

Lily   He could be British! . . . Four drowned British have washed up on that beach this year. You heard that plane go down . . . It could be him.

Jeanne   It went down at eight o' clock this morning into the dark, cold sea. Be serious. If he's found here, they'll shoot *me*, as head of the household; do you understand?

Lily   Nobody saw us bringing him here . . .

Jeanne   You are a *stupid* woman! I can't believe you're putting yourself in such danger! You know your situation here . . .

Lily   What do you mean?

Jeanne   I mean, if they find out what you are!

Lily   How can they? No one knows, except you.

Jeanne   (*pause*) Why did you drag Estelle into this?

Lily   Lake wouldn't come with me. I had to help him, Mrs Becquet.

Jeanne   Why?

Lily   . . . He looks like Myles.

Jeanne   (*pause*) Do what you like. If he dies, dump him back on the beach where you found him. Living or dead, I want him out of here before it's bright. I'm going to bed. I don't want my daughter upset, and I don't want to see him.

Lily runs outside. Jeanne pours herself a drink. She drinks it. She pours another. She exits. The door opens and Lily and Estelle enter, dragging a man between

*them. He's naked except for an old coat. Bits of straw
fall off him.*

Lily Get him over to the fire.

Estelle He made a noise.

Lily When?

Estelle In the barn. Like a 'b' and air going through his
mouth.

Lily That's good.

Estelle Then he puked up.

Lily Oh.

Estelle All salt water and yellow stuff.

Lily Oh.

Estelle And he moaned but I couldn't tell what language.

Lily Put him in the chair . . .

*They lay him down in an armchair in front of the
stove. They take a moment to get their breath back.
Lily opens the stove doors and puts some fuel on.*

Estelle Look at him.

Lily (*pause*). Estelle, run upstairs and find all the blankets
you can. Bring him the pillows off my bed and the spare
eiderdown. And find him something to wear. We have to
get him warm.

Estelle What are you going to do?

Lily I'm going to make him drink something.

Estelle Do you want me to go and get Dr Brown?

Lily Dr Brown works for the Krauts.

Estelle So does Mummy.

Lily No she doesn't, not in that way. No doctors, we can't risk it.

Lily goes to pour a glass of Cognac. Estelle gazes at the man. She touches his face.

Lily Stop gawping Estelle. Get the blankets.

Estelle exits. Lily puts the Cognac to the man's lips. He chokes and splutters.

Lily Drink, come on, drink. You're somewhere warm. You're out of the dark, now. Don't die bloke, live . . .

Lily moves to kiss him on the lips. As she does so, the lights go out, leaving the kitchen in total darkness, except for the firelight coming from the stove. Lily starts with the shock.

Lily (*to the man*) Stay there. I'm going to find a light.

Lily fumbles towards the kitchen table. She searches for matches.

Estelle (*calling, off*) Lily! Turn the lights back on!

Lily I can't can I? The power's gone! . . .

Lily lights the lamp. Estelle comes in, staggering under an armful of blankets and linen.

Estelle I hate this house . . . . I hit my knee on the landing.

Lily Make him a bed there, near the stove, and we'll lift him on to it.

Estelle It's stone. It'll be too cold!

Lily Then make it on the table.

Estelle I brought him this to wear. It's Daddy's old one.

Estelle throws an old-fashioned night shirt at Lily.

Lily Blimey . . . Turn round and I'll put it on him.

Estelle turns round. She takes the eiderdown and spreads it over the table. Lily takes off the man's coat and puts the night shirt on him. They both work rapidly.

Lily Estelle.

Estelle What?

Lily When you came in and saw your mum and that Major, what did you . . . I mean, you looked like you'd seen a ghost.

Estelle So?

Lily What were they doing?

Estelle Nothing.

Lily So . . . did you just get a fright?

Estelle All this hate came up and blocked my throat.

Lily Have you seen him before?

Estelle No, I just *hate* him. (*Gazing at the man.*) He's got cuts on his legs.

Lily Oh . . . He must've hit them on the rocks.

Estelle There's barbed wire in the sea.

Lily (*pause*) I should clean them, or something, shouldn't I?

Estelle Yes.

Lily Estelle, I don't like this. He's too still.

Estelle He's just sleeping, isn't he?

Lily (*puts her head to his chest*) He's hardly breathing. I can't hear his heart.

Estelle Move the table over there.

Lily   Right. Yes.

They move the table. Estelle makes sure it's right above her square of power.

Estelle   It'll help him. It's on a square of power.

Lily   (*to the man*) Come on, live.

Estelle   Pick him up, Lily!

Lily   (*on the verge of tears*) LIVE!

Estelle   I'll get his legs.

They pick the man up and manage to get him on to the table. Estelle immediately lies down next to him. She puts her arms and one leg around him.

Lily   What are you doing?

Estelle   I'm warming him with my body heat. I'm going to save his life. You put the blankets over us.

Lily   You can't do that!

Estelle   Why not?

Lily   That's not what you do!

Estelle   It's how you save people in the Alps.

Lily   How d'you know?

Estelle   I read it.

Lily   We should be doing something! . . . Those cuts on his legs –

Estelle   Turn him to his side so if he pukes up in the night, he won't choke on it.

They turn him.

Estelle   These girls were on a skiing trip from their Swiss finishing school and an avalanche blocked off their route so they hugged each other all night to stay warm. But there was one stuck-up girl who wouldn't touch anybody and she went off by herself. Soon, she found herself sinking into the snow and all she wanted to do was sleep and sleep. In the morning the others were rescued but the stuck-up girl was frozen in a block of ice.

Lily Right.

Estelle Cause that's what happens when you die of cold; you fall into a deeper and deeper sleep and if no one warms you up with their body heat like your friends or a St Bernard, you go further and further inside yourself into a land of dreams and eventually your spirit leaves your body and floats up to the firmament. It'll go all over me now.

Lily What?

Estelle If he pukes. I'm changing sides.

Lily Right . . .

Lily piles quilts and blankets over Estelle and the man.

Estelle (*through the blankets*) I can hear his heart.

Lily Good . . .

Lily puts the lamp on a nearby chair. Then she squeezes on to the other side of the table.

Estelle What are you doing?

Lily Same as you, what d'you think?

Lily curls up against the man. She puts her head to his chest.

Estelle He smells of the sea, doesn't he? How long do you think he was in there?

Lily I don't know. I think the mermaids must've rescued him.

Estelle   Have you ever heard the story about the Guernsey girl and the Fairy King?

Lily   No.

Estelle   This Guernsey girl is walking down by the sea and she sees this man, fast asleep on the beach. She tries to waken him but she can't, so she kisses him. Well, with her kiss he wakes, and they fall instantly in love. He turns out to be the King of Fairyland and he takes her there to be his Queen. When they get there, the other fairies are so jealous, that they all run away from Fairyland so they can marry Guernsey girls too. When the Fairy King finds out, he's really angry. He forces them to kiss their brides goodbye and go back home. But nine months later the girls have babies. And the people of Guernsey are changed forever because now they have fairy blood. And that's true. The people of Guernsey have fairy blood.

Lily   Well. That's what you call it then.

Estelle   It reminds me of this.

Lily   How?

Estelle   Finding him on the beach.

Lily   I'm not a Guernsey girl, am I?

Estelle   No, but I am.

Lily   (*smiling*) Oh I see . . .

Estelle   Can we call him something.?

Lily   If you like. We could call him George, after the King.

Estelle   (*shyly*) Gabriel.

Lily   Why d'you want to call him that?

Estelle   It's my favourite name.

Lily   Blimey.

Estelle   Wake up, Gabriel.

Estelle kisses him. Pause.

Lily   No luck, Guernsey girl . . . You'd better go to bed now.

Estelle   No! . . .

Lily   You should've been asleep hours ago, come on.

Estelle   I want to stay!

Lily   You can't, Estelle . . .

Estelle   Why not? (*Pause.*) He won't die; I *know* he won't! Don't make me go to bed!

Lily   I promised your mother.

Estelle   Lily, Please! You need me to keep this side of him warm . . . Mummy doesn't have to know; I can go upstairs in the morning, before she gets up! . . . Please!

Lily   You have to go.

Estelle   It's NOT FAIR! Nobody ever lets me do *anything*! (*Getting out of bed, fighting her tears.*) I'm not telling you my plan now . . .

Lily   What plan?

Estelle   To get The Hermitage back! And if he dies it's your fault!

Lily   Come on Estelle.

Estelle   Everybody *hates* me! . . .

Estelle leaves. Lily sighs. She looks at the man.

Lily   Gabriel.

She curls herself around him. She doesn't close her eyes.

Scene Two

A sunny afternoon, two days later. An attic room with a small window. A large stock of black market goods has been laid to one side and a makeshift bed set up. Gabriel lies in it, unconscious. Jeanne is glancing through an old magazine. After a while, she puts it down. She looks deeply troubled. She sighs.

Jeanne For heaven's sake, woman. It's just a bloody dream.

She stands and lights a cigarette. She looks at Gabriel.

Jeanne Oh I'm sorry, do you mind if I smoke?

Jeanne leans over Gabriel and blows smoke in his face.

Jeanne Well, Little German Boy, we're all getting thoroughly bored. (*She shakes him, irritated. She moves away.*) Mrs Lake seems to think I should talk to you. I think it's a waste of time, myself. It's uninspiring, talking to the dead. If I was at all fatalistic, I'd say you were *sent* here to – . It sounds absurd. When the time comes, would you rather be buried or cremated? Because if it was up to me I'd throw you back in the sea, right now . . . and I'm not afraid of my cruelty, only my cowardice. I can't sleep with you in my house. I'm having nightmares. I want you gone. (*Pause. Jeanne touches his forehead.*) You poor boy . . . Marooned in a house full of bitches.

Jeanne hears someone approaching. She immediately sits down and opens the magazine. Lake comes in with a tray of soup.

Lake I made him some soup.

Jeanne   He won't eat it, will he?

Lake   No.

Jeanne   Then why bother?

Lake   He might like the taste of it on his lips.

Jeanne   It's a waste.

Lake   My kitchen, my soup. (*To Gabriel.*) Hello my angel! It's Mrs Lake! (*To Jeanne.*) Have you been talking to him?

Jeanne   No.

Lake   You should talk to him.

Jeanne   I don't expect he understands.

Lake   That's not the point. He needs friendly voices.

Jeanne   Does he now?

Lake   Friendly voices help.

Jeanne   How do you know?

Lake   I brought him out of that fever, didn't I? That fever would have killed him.

Jeanne   Drugs brought him out of that fever; black market drugs that I paid for.

Lake   (*to Gabriel*) Well then, my lamb, you're going to help Mrs Lake now, aren't you? You're going to eat up all this soup she made you!

Jeanne   I've got a fear Margaret . . . I've felt this . . . dread the last two days and I can't sleep. I can't sleep and when I do I have these ghastly nightmares, so vivid I think there's blood on my hands –

Lake   Shut up. (*To Gabriel.*) There we are. Lovely mashed swede and a bit of chopped up Spam . . .

Jeanne   Don't tell me to shut up. I pay your wages.

Lake   Black market pays my wages. I don't want him hearing things like that. It'll trouble him.

Jeanne   If he's troubled, Margaret, don't you think it's because you're trying to asphyxiate him with soup?

Lake   He wants the taste of it on his lips.

Jeanne   How do you know what he wants? He's a cretin, not a baby boy.

Lily   (*entering*) Mrs Becquet! . . . There's a bunch of Krauts in front of The Hermitage. They've got Estelle. That Major from the other night – he's holding on to her.

Jeanne   (*going to the window*) What's happened? What's she done?

Lily   I don't know. I just saw it out my bedroom window.

Jeanne   Well . . . I expect the Major has finally discovered we're a cow-free farm. (*To Lake.*) Margaret, get your coat.

Lake   I'll stay here and watch him.

Lily   I'll watch him.

Lake   (*defensively*) He's having his soup.

Lily   (*in horror, noticing*) What are you doing to him?

Lake   Sustenance.

Lily   He can't eat that. It looks like sick!

Lake   It's wholesome, nourishing food.

Jeanne   Margaret, I want you with me, right now. Please don't leave my side.

   Jeanne leaves.

Lake   Feed him that soup.

Lily   You must be joking.

Lake   Then it's your fault if he dies.

Lily   I saved his life!

Lake leaves. Lily takes a napkin from Lake's tray and wipes Gabriel's face.

Lily   Cow-free farm. I can think of at least two cows living here. Wicked old bag; what's she done to you? . . . Evil-looking slop. There. This is what happens when I leave you. I'm sorry. I had to get some sleep. (*Lily goes to the window.*) There they go. Flying up the lane on their bloody broomsticks. (*Pause.*) It's not even eight miles long, this island. I can cycle round it in half a day. And I've grown to hate it, Gabriel. I hate every rock. I want to smash every stupid little garden and prissy little house. I've lived such a *useless* life here, up to my ankles in chicken shit, growing bloody veg for them to flog to the Krauts. If only I was in London or France or anywhere, I could be *doing something*! The whole world's in chaos and I'm stuck in bloody fairyland. (*Returning to the bed.*) I nearly ran over you on my bike. I was in a right state; you scared the living daylights out of me. I was out celebrating my anniversary, you see. In the minefields. Three years to the day since I came here as a bride. 'Guernsey's one of the island jewels of Europe,' he'd say. 'They'll love you there,' and he'd look at me and laugh 'til I cracked up too. When we got here . . . I shouldn't tell you. (*Pause.*) 'Lily's my Jew-girl,' first thing he said, and he gives me this great, long kiss right in front of her. It was like he . . . Still. Three months I had with him, that's all. I can hardly remember it now. (*Touches him.*) They're softer than mine, your hands. Mine are ruined, picking sprouts out o' the frost.

Pause. She kisses Gabriel on the lips.

Lily (*whispers*) Please don't be a madman. Please don't be a Kraut. Please wake up and be my friend. (*No response. To herself.*) Stupid cow.

She goes to the window again. During the following, Gabriel opens his eyes. For a while he's too bewildered to move, but he gradually begins to focus on Lily. He slowly sits up.

Lily What's it like, flying? What's it like cutting right through the clouds and soaring into the sun? I can't imagine how beautiful everything must look from up there. The very thought of being above the clouds, above the clouds in all that light; it's beyond me . . . makes me want to cry, just thinking about it. (*Pause.*) I get these attacks Gabriel, where I start going mad inside cause I can't get away. Feels like I can't breathe. Sometimes, when I'm in the fields all alone and the sky's pressing down, or in the lane where the white weeds grow, it gets on top of me so much, all the green and the clouds and the smell, that I shut my eyes and with all the force of my person I say: Give me wings so I could rise up off my feet, so I could strive away and see this place fading in the distance. . . Give me wings so I could see the sea stretching out beneath me, all blue, all dazzling, and I think, that feeling, that feeling I want, of freedom of floating, that feeling . . . that'd be worth dying for, wouldn't it? (*She is crying.*) Oh! . . . I was going to walk right into those mines and blow myself to kingdom come! . . . I would've done it too but I'm glad I didn't now, and I owe that to –

Lily turns around. Gabriel is staring at her, bewildered. She starts with shock. Pause.

Lily You're awake.

Lily wipes her eyes. She goes to the bed.

Lily   I don't know what to say. You're awake. Can you speak? Do you understand me?

Gabriel   I thought I was dead.

Lily   Oh . . .

Gabriel   I couldn't focus. It was a blur, light and colours; I thought I was –

Lily   (*taking his hand and gripping it tightly*) No . . . you're not dead. See? Your hands are warmer than mine. (*Smiling with joy.*) English . . . You're him, aren't you? The man in the plane . . .

Gabriel   (*pause*) Who are you?

Lily   I'm Lilian Becquet. Lily.

Gabriel   Where am I?

Lily   You're at the Lodge on the Hermitage estate. It's a farm near St Saviours. On Guernsey . . . The island of Guernsey. What's your name?

Gabriel   I need some water.

Lily   Here . . .

Lily gives Gabriel some water.

Gabriel   Thank you. (*He drinks.*) I can't remember.

Lily   You can't remember your name? (*Pause.*) Can you remember anything?

Gabriel   No.

Lily   Well . . . you've only just woken up. It's the shock I expect. What you've been through's made you forget.

Gabriel   What happened to me?

Lily   Your plane crashed into the sea.

Gabriel My plane.

Lily I was down by the beach three nights ago and I saw you lying on the sand. It looked like you'd dragged yourself out of the waves. At first I thought you were dead, then you moved your hand. Your fingers uncurled . . .

Gabriel You saved me?

Lily Yes. Me and the people who live here.

Gabriel Did I say anything?

Lily No, you weren't able. You've been ill for three days. Unconscious. We thought you were going to die, Gabriel. It's a miracle –

Gabriel What did you call me?

Lily Oh. Gabriel.

Gabriel You said you didn't know my name.

Lily We made it up. We had to call you something.

Gabriel Gabriel?

Lily My sister-in-law chose it; she's only ten.

Gabriel (*panicking*) I can't remember anything.

Lily Please, don't panic.

Gabriel I don't know what I look like. I have no memory of myself at all.

Lily Wait, there's a mirror here . . .

She hands Gabriel a mirror. He looks at himself, concentrated, but unrecognising.

Gabriel I don't know who this is . . .

He puts the mirror down, troubled.

Lily You should rest.

Gabriel   No, I must think, think –

Lily   If you panic, you'll drive all your thoughts away!

Gabriel   Think; my name!

Lily   (*firmly*) Just relax. The essence of you is here. The essence of you, the person. You're alive. You've survived. Give yourself time.

Gabriel   Yes.

Lily   Rest . . . and think calmly. Anything, any image in your head, no matter how small . . . Hold on to it and the rest will follow, I know it will.

Gabriel   (*pause*) Falling.

Lily   What?

Gabriel   Darkness. Falling . . .

Lily   You remember falling?

Gabriel nods.

Lily   I expect you bailed out of your plane, got your parachute off in the sea . . .

Gabriel   No. Falling.

Lily   I don't know what you mean.

Gabriel   No plane, no parachute. I was free. (*Pause.*) Why were you crying?

Lily   I wasn't crying. (*Looking down.*) I'm not like that, Gabriel.

Gabriel   Not like what?

Lily   I never cry. (*Looking up.*) Would you like something to eat?

Gabriel   Yes, yes, I'm hungry . . . I'm starving! . . .

Lily   Right. I'll get you some food. Promise me you won't worry while I'm gone.

Gabriel   I promise . . .

Lily   I'll be back in five minutes.

Lily stands to move away. Gabriel takes hold of her hand.

Gabriel   Tell me your name again.

Lily   Lily.

Gabriel   Lily. Thank you.

<h1 style="text-align:center">Scene Three</h1>

The kitchen, a short while later. During the course of the scene, evening falls. By the end, it's almost dark. Lily is at the table rapidly making Spam sandwiches. She is humming as she works, in high spirits. Suddenly Estelle enters, breathless, afraid.

Estelle   Hide me!!

Lily   What's happened?

Estelle   Mummy's going to murder me . . .

Lily   Estelle, what've you done?

Estelle   The Major wants to put me in jail!

Lily   What for? . . .

Estelle   (*in terror*) Hide me, she's coming! . . .

Lily   Go in the cupboard. I'll see if I can calm her down.

Estelle   He wants to send me to a prison camp . . .

Lily   Well it's against the law to send children to prison camps, so he was having you on, wasn't he? Come on, quick.

Lily holds the cupboard door open. Estelle hands her a small book.

Estelle   You have to take this.

Lily   What is it?

Estelle   It's his. I stole it.

Lily   You did not.

Estelle   I did. It's his diary. You can destroy a person when you know their secrets.

Lily   (*flicking through it*) Estelle, it's in German.

Estelle   (*disappointed*) Is it?

Lily   Course it is; he's a Kraut, isn't he?

Estelle   I didn't look . . .

Lily   How could you be so stupid? He'll know you've taken it –

Estelle   (*disappearing into the cupboard*) Shut me in!

Lily   And he's going to come looking for it, isn't he?

Estelle   Shut me in!!

Lily shuts Estelle in the cupboard. She looks frantically round the kitchen.

Lily   Oh bloody hell! . . .

She shoves the book in the bread bin, just as Jeanne enters, furious, almost crying.

Jeanne   Where is she?

Lily   Who?

Jeanne   Estelle!

Lily   I don't know.

Jeanne   I saw her come in here!

Lily   You can't have done . . .

Jeanne   Where is she then?

Lily   Maybe she went in the barn. What's she done?

Jeanne   (*close to tears*) She has *embarrassed* me!

Lily   Oh dear.

Jeanne I'll *murder* her when I get my hands on her! Of all the *stupid* games to play!

Lake Get me a drink, quick.

Jeanne (*turning on Lake*) You're too fat; that's all that's wrong with you!

Lake Don't. I need a drink.

Jeanne (*going to fill a glass of Cognac*) I should never have bought you with me. You're a liability.

Lake You were damn glad I was there. You're scared of that man.

Jeanne Don't be ridiculous.

Lake Why be scared of him?

Jeanne I'm not.

Lake You were flirting. Only ever seen you flirt when you're scared.

Jeanne I have never flirted in my life.

Lily Is he coming here?

Jeanne (*handing Lake the drink*) No.

Lily Good.

Jeanne He was going to but I put him off. I had to *prostitute* myself.

Lily How?

Jeanne (*sighs*) I offered to show him the Neolithic tombs.

Lily Well . . . that's not so bad is it?

Jeanne You go with him then! You spend the day with that *reptile*.

Lily   What happened, Mrs Becquet?

Jeanne   Estelle's been breaking in there.

Lake   She's been haunting them.

Lily   Pardon?

Lake   Creeping into The Hermitage and haunting them.

Lily   Why?

Jeanne   It's her plan, she says, to get the place back; so utterly ridiculous I'm ashamed.

Lily   What's she been doing?

Jeanne   You know the kind of thing; banging doors in empty rooms, moving things every time they put them down –

Lake   She made a blood stain in the morning room.

Lily   No.

Lake   Every time they cleaned it up, she put it back again.

Jeanne   It's gone on for three days. And then they catch her and she behaves *ridiculously*. Shouting hysterical rubbish like Joan of bloody Arc.

Lily   What did they do?

Jeanne   They laughed.

Lily   So they thought it was funny?

Jeanne   I said they laughed; it's not the same thing.

Lily   But they took it well? (*Giggles.*) They really thought they had a ghost?

Lake   Oh you got to hand it to her, she was clever. She picked on that clockwork monkey Major – tied a thread to his picture of Hitler and pulled it off the mantelpiece right in front of him. Went straight in the fire; all shattered everywhere. She put dead mice all over his floor from every trap in the house.

Jeanne   And the little savage scratched words into the panelling on his wall.

Lake   Wrote 'You're in your coffin.'

Jeanne   He won't forget this.

Lily   You're in your coffin? . . .

Jeanne   Or forgive it. (*Pause.*) I'm an idiot. She's with the madman in the attic, isn't she?

Lily   No.

Jeanne   I'm going up.

Lily   No! You can't . . . He's awake.

Lake   Lord Jesus . . .

Lily   Don't go up; he doesn't know who you are.

Jeanne   Why didn't you tell us?

Lily   I was just about to.

Jeanne   So. The vegetable wakes. Is he capable of speech or do we have a drooling half-wit on our hands?

Lily   He can speak.

Jeanne   German or English?

Lily   He's English. And he's quite lovely actually; quite a gentleman. I should take this food up now. I told him I'd only leave him for a minute.

Jeanne   So who is he then? What's his story?

Lake   I'll go up.

Jeanne   If anyone goes up it'll be me! What's his story?

Lily   Well . . . he hasn't got one as a matter of fact.

Jeanne   Of course he's got one.

Lily   He's lost his memory.

Jeanne   Oh. How convenient.

Lily   It's not his fault.

Lake   He can't remember anything?

Lily   Nothing, not even his name. I mean, after all he's been through, he's probably in shock, isn't he?

Jeanne   But he strikes you as perfectly sane?

Lily   Yes.

Jeanne   (*sitting, relieved*) Well . . . thank God he's not going to die here. (*Pause.*) So, he's alive and awake and now, thank God, we can get rid of him. Margaret, go down to the village.

Lake   You can't get rid of him just like that!

Jeanne   I can and I will. Now that he's awake, he can walk away on his own two feet, and he's going, this afternoon.

Lake   I want to see him first.

Lily   You'll disturb him.

Lake   Course I won't disturb him; he's my boy!

Jeanne   No! Margaret, please. We've done our bit; we've saved his life. Go down to the village and talk to the crones –

Lake   Why should I? No one'll help. You're not liked or trusted; who am I supposed to ask?

Jeanne I know you know people. You know everyone! Get someone in your coven to take him in.

Lake Oh!

Jeanne Margaret, help me. Please, I beg you. I want him out of my house!

Lake looks at her. Pause. She walks out, leaving the door wide open.

Lily Mrs Becquet, if you were to talk to him –

Jeanne Just get him ready to leave.

There's a crash inside the cupboard. Jeanne looks furiously at Lily and opens the door. She pulls Estelle out. Estelle runs for the stairs. Jeanne grabs her by the hair.

Estelle Ow!

Jeanne Did you think you'd get away with it?!

Estelle I want to see him!

Jeanne You little – !

Jeanne pulls Estelle towards her, viciously.

Estelle Gabriel!

Jeanne Did you think if you hid long enough I'd *forget*?

Estelle Aaahh!

Jeanne This is the end of your freedom. From now on, you WILL NOT LEAVE THIS YARD!

Estelle Mummy, no! . . .

Jeanne (*slapping her*) You have *humiliated* me! Do you know what you've done? Do you *know*?

Estelle I didn't mean it!

Jeanne   How could you be so *stupid*? Those men are not to be toyed with or played with! They are Nazi officers!

Von Pfunz appears in the doorway. He watches.

Estelle   They took our house!

Jeanne slaps Estelle. Estelle howls.

Jeanne   They're the occupying power! They can take any damn thing they like! I have fought for years to keep good relations with them and you have *ruined it*!

Lily   Stop it, please!

Jeanne   Do you think the Major's just going to forget it? Do you?

Estelle   I don't know!

Jeanne   NO HE'S NOT! He's going to MAKE US PAY! Because of *you*, I have to spend a whole day with that twisted *death's head*, showing him round the bloody (*Slap.*) ruins! (*Slap.*)

Estelle   (*bawling*) I'm sorry! . . .

Jeanne   Why did you (*Slap.*) do it? You *know* what's at stake!!

Estelle   I wanted to do something *brave* . . .

Lily   It's not her fault! I put her up to it!

Jeanne is just about to round on Lily when she notices Von Pfunz. Lily turns to see him. Jeanne releases Estelle. A horrified silence. Estelle smothers her sobs.

Von Pfunz   Good afternoon.

Jeanne   Major. How nice to see you again.

Von Pfunz   Excuse me for disturbing your peace. I wish to talk to the little lady. (*Pause. To Lily.*) How is sick cow?

Lily Oh . . . much better thank you. It's gone back to its proper owner now. We were looking after it for another farmer, you see.

Von Pfunz Oh?

Lily He was . . . having a new roof put on his barn. So we took his cow for him. Anyway it's gone now.

Von Pfunz (*he giggles*) Fan*tas*tic.

Jeanne Won't you come in?

Von Pfunz enters the kitchen, neatly closing the door behind him.

Jeanne Would you like a cup of tea?

Von Pfunz No thank you.

Jeanne (*going to the bread bin*) Perhaps I can tempt you with one of Mrs Lake's flapjacks?

Von Pfunz Extremely hospitable, but –

Jeanne Sometimes in our kitchen, you'd barely know there was a war on.

Von Pfunz I have come to speak with the little lady.

Jeanne (*pause*) You've picked a bad moment. You'll have to call back.

Von Pfunz Forgive me but I prefer to speak with her now. Alone, thank you.

Estelle I've already said sorry.

Von Pfunz It's not an apology I seek. Really, I find them tedious and I know in truth, you are not sorry at all.

Estelle I am.

Von Pfunz Only for being caught. In my more detached moments, I must admit I find what you did extremely 'spirited', if I may make such an obvious pun, and also rather funny. Don't you agree, Jeanne?

Jeanne   No.

Von Pfunz   It is always a joke to torment those who are sleeping.

Jeanne   She has been punished, Major, as you can see.

Von Pfunz   Punishment has never been an attractive ethic to me, ladies, for the simple reason that it doesn't work. When a person believes they've committed no offence, no amount of punishment will make them *feel* their crime. (*Glancing at Lily.*) And so many times, the mistake is made of punishing the innocent while the guilty go free. No. Punishment creates only martyrs.

Gabriel enters, breathless and weak on his feet, a white sheet wrapped around him. The women look at him, aghast.

Lily   Gabriel. What are you doing out of bed?

Gabriel   I heard crying . . . . I had to come down. (*Dizzy.*) Oh . . . excuse me . . .

Lily helps Gabriel to a chair.

Jeanne   This is my nephew, Major – Gabriel Lascalles. He's . . . recovering from flu.

Gabriel   (*to Estelle*) Are you all right?

Estelle nods, completely overawed.

Gabriel   Did you fall over? Are you hurt?

Estelle shakes her head, slowly.

Jeanne   Gabriel, this is Major Von Pfunz of the German army.

Gabriel   How do you do?

Gabriel politely holds out his hand, completely unperturbed by Von Pfunz's uniform.

Von Pfunz   (*shaking Gabriel's hand*) Very nice pleasure, yes.

Gabriel   Deutsch. Eigentlich sind doch englisch und deutch sprachverwandt. Manche sind der Meinung, daß deutsch hart klingt, aber ich finde, es hat eine bestimmte Ausdruckskraft und schönheit ganz für sich. Es ist die Sprache dunkler Wälder und kalter Winter; die Sprache eines schaffenden Volkes. Natürlich offenbart sich die deutsche Seele wahrhaftig erst in deutscher Musik . . . (*German. It's the sister language to English, isn't it? People say it's harsh but I think it has a strength and a beauty entirely of it's own. It's the language of dark forests and cold winters; the language of a people who strive. Of course it's German music that really illuminates the German soul . . .*)

Von Pfunz   Und die Seele der Briten durch die Dicht-kunst. (*And poetry that illuminates the British.*)

Gabriel   Da haben Sie wohl recht. (*I suppose you're right.*)

Von Pfunz   Sie sprechen ein ausgezeichnetes Deutsch, Herr Lascalles. (*You speak excellent German, Mr Lascalles.*)

Gabriel   Tatsächlich? (*Do I?*)

Von Pfunz   Als sei es ihre Muttersprache. Kein Akzent und nichts . . . (*Like a native. No trace of an accent at all . . .*)

Gabriel   (*puzzled*) Oh . . .

Jeanne   Gabriel is my brother's boy, from Torteval. He's recovering from a jolly bad fever. The air on this part of the island is so much better . . . His parents insisted he come.

Gabriel I'm sorry about the state of me. I couldn't find any clothes.

Lily You shouldn't be out of bed.

Jeanne He's been delirious. Lilian dear, why don't you take him upstairs?

Lily Come on, I made you this food.

Lily takes the tray and goes to the door. Gabriel stands.

Gabriel (*to Jeanne*) Am I really your brother's boy?

Jeanne Of course you are, dear.

Gabriel (*puzzled*) . . . Then you know who I am?

Jeanne Of course I do! . . . You've been very ill. Your poor parents have been so worried.

Gabriel Well . . . thank you. (*To Von Pfunz.*) Warum tragen Sie eigentlich diese Uniform? (*Why are you wearing that uniform?*)

Von Pfunz Sie sagt ihnen nichts? (*You don't recognise it?*)

Gabriel Ich fürchte nein. (*I'm afraid not.*)

Von Pfunz Dann haben Sie ein sehr beschütztes Leben gelebt. (*Then you've lived a very sheltered life.*)

Gabriel Schick ist sie ja. (*It's very smart.*)

Von Pfunz Danke schön. (*Thank you . . .*)

Gabriel Was bedeuted dies alles? (*What is it?*)

Lily Gabriel! . . .

Gabriel Sorry. Excuse me.

Gabriel exits with Lily. The light is beginning to fade.

Jeanne He's been terribly ill, the poor boy. It was touch and go for a while . . .

Von Pfunz   Do you know, he asked me what my uniform was.

Jeanne   Really?

Von Pfunz   He didn't recognise it.

Jeanne   I think the fever must have temporarily affected his mind. I mean (*She laughs.*) he didn't recognise me, either . . .

Von Pfunz   Extraordinary, isn't it? He was telling me how much he admires German music, how it illuminates the German soul. Tell me, what does he do for a living?

Jeanne   . . . He works on his father's farm.

Von Pfunz   A man of his education? He speaks German like a native.

Jeanne   Well, it's the war you see . . . it's rather clipped his wings. He was actually educated at Oxford, specialising in modern languages but when war broke out he was stranded here. Tragedy, really. He longed to be in the RAF, like Myles. He . . . had a broken leg you see, which he contracted when his horse threw him on a cliff path. He was in traction when they were evacuating men of military age. The occupation has prevented him from fulfilling his potential because he refuses to work for the enemy. He helps on his father's farm. Maurice Lascalles and Son of Torteval. Vegetables. (*Pause.*) They grew orchids and carnations before the war but of course, demand has dropped.

Von Pfunz   May I see his papers?

Jeanne   Certainly. His father has them in Torteval. I can send Mrs Lake over for them tomorrow, while we're sightseeing. Would that be convenient?

Von Pfunz   It thrills me to hear you lie, Jeanne. Every word excites me. To hear you lie when I know you are capable of speaking such truth . . .

Estelle   That is the truth! He's my cousin Gabriel from Torteval and if you don't believe it you can jolly well jump!

Von Pfunz   Well! The poltergeist . . . I had almost forgotten about our *tête à tête*.

Jeanne   What do you want her for, Major?

Von Pfunz   I discover that she has taken something from my room.

Jeanne   What?

Estelle   Nothing.

Jeanne   She says she hasn't taken anything.

Von Pfunz   I'm afraid she's lying. Where can she have learnt such behaviour?

Jeanne   I can't leave you with her, I'm sorry.

Estelle   I'm not scared of him, Mummy.

Von Pfunz   What do you think I will do? Hit her? I have never hit a child . . .

Jeanne   (*to Estelle*) I'll be in my room. You only have to call.

 Jeanne exits.

Von Pfunz   You know what I want.

Estelle   No.

Von Pfunz   Come on, little phantom; you have a book of mine.

Estelle   No I don't.

Von Pfunz   I would like it back.

Estelle   I haven't got it.

Von Pfunz   Don't waste my time, please.

Estelle   I don't know what you're talking about. Sorry.

Von Pfunz   I ask you kindly to return it.

Estelle   I can't, can I?

Von Pfunz   That book is my only friend and I am a lonely man.

Estelle   I haven't got it.

Von Pfunz   I'm irritated by lies. I respect only the truth.

Estelle   That is the truth.

Von Pfunz   (*pause*) Estelle, I wish to make it clear that you are in *very deep trouble*. When I said at The Hermitage that I could have you imprisoned for what you've done, I wasn't making a joke.

Estelle   You can't put children in prison; it's against the law.

Von Pfunz   So. There is something essential about the war, that you have failed to grasp: whoever is winning, and that is us, can do what they like. War is governed by force and chaos, not the law. This is a real war Estelle, not some stupid game in your head. Over the water millions of people are dying. It is out of control. Force and chaos are terrible masters. I have killed people, yes I have, an ordinary man like me. If you had known me before the war you would have said Von Pfunz? He is a nice fellow, a good old chap but now, imagine, I could kill you. There is no justice left, only force. If you were a little Polish girl or a Jew and you had taken my book, I would take you outside the door right now and shoot you in the back of the head (*He touches her; she flinches.*) and no one would say a word.

Estelle   Maybe you just lost it in your room . . .

Von Pfunz   (*moves away, irritated*) Did you give it to your sister-in-law?

Estelle   No.

Von Pfunz   I think you did. Perhaps I should take her outside and shoot her instead?

Estelle   She hasn't done anything!

Von Pfunz   She is the evil mind behind you. I heard her say so herself.

Estelle   She was lying!

Von Pfunz   So are you!! (*Pause. Calmer.*) Where are the lights in here?

Estelle points. Von Pfunz flicks the switch. Nothing happens.

Estelle   There's no power.

Von Pfunz   People will laugh at you for taking my book. Do you know what is in there? There are no state secrets or Nazi plans. Do you know what it is that I write? I am a poet; does that surprise you? (*He giggles.*) I hardly think you're going to bring about the fall of the Third Reich with my poetry book . . .

Estelle   I haven't got it.

Von Pfunz   (*lighting candles*) What about your handsome cousin? Has he got it?

Estelle   No.

Von Pfunz   Shall I ask him?

Estelle   He's not well.

Von Pfunz   How old is he?

Estelle   Twenty-six. His birthday's the fifth of August.

Von Pfunz   Why do you lie Estelle?

Estelle   I'm not lying.

Von Pfunz   Has your Mummy got my book?

Estelle   No.

Von Pfunz   Perhaps you wouldn't trust her with it? Perhaps you think she spends too much time with Germans?

Estelle   No.

Von Pfunz   Do you like her spending time with us?

Estelle   Don't care.

Von Pfunz   Do you like her selling food to us while the islanders are hungry? She's a parasite, don't you think? . . . Would you like to see her going to jail?

Estelle   She hasn't done anything!

Von Pfunz   What had I done to you, when you stole my book!? What had I done to you when you leant over me in the night and put those *things* on my face? When I woke in that *horrible* way did you listen to my fear and *laugh*? Did my anguish *amuse* you?

Estelle   No.

Von Pfunz   Why did you do that to me?

Estelle   Don't know.

Von Pfunz   Why not one of the other men? We are all the same.

Estelle   No you're not.

Von Pfunz   We're all the enemy.

Estelle   None of them talk to you! They all leave the lounge when you go in. They don't like you!

Von Pfunz   Then we have something in common. (*Leaning over her.*) Forgive me, but no one likes you either, do they? You have the haunted look of a child who is lonely. A child who must imagine her friends out of thin air, communing with the ghosts. Perhaps they are your only real friends, the shades of night. It will always be that way. Do you understand me Estelle? I know exactly the kind of woman you will become . . . unloved. (*He caresses her face.*) You are in your coffin.

Estelle   (*attempting to turn her head*) Excuse me.

Von Pfunz   Don't you like to hear the truth?

Estelle   (*close to tears*) Your breath smells.

Von Pfunz   (*gripping her face, hard*) That is enough. Give me my book.

Estelle   I threw it in the sea!

Von Pfunz   (*shaking her furiously*) You're lying, idiot child! LYING!

Estelle   Mummy! MUMMY!

Von Pfunz   Damn you!

> *Estelle screams. He releases her. Jeanne enters, flicking the lights on. They work.*

Estelle   He said you were a parasite. He wants to shoot Lily and put you in jail!

Jeanne   Of course he doesn't. He's making nasty, idle threats.

Jeanne   Perhaps you'd go now.

Von Pfunz   I don't yet have what I came for.

Jeanne   And what's that?

Von Pfunz   My book.

Jeanne   Give the Major his book!

Estelle   I haven't got it!

Jeanne   Is that the truth?

Estelle   Yes!

Jeanne   Then go to your room.

Von Pfunz   I must have this settled!

Jeanne   If she's got it, you'll get it back. You can rely
on me.

Estelle exits. Pause.

Von Pfunz   I'm so looking forward to our trip tomorrow,
Jeanne. I was thinking, perhaps we could visit your
nephew's farm on the way.

Jeanne   It's not on our route.

Von Pfunz   A pity; he's so charming. I was hoping he'd
come with us.

Jeanne   . . . I'm afraid he's too unwell.

Von Pfunz   How old is he?

Jeanne   He must be . . . twenty-five.

Von Pfunz   Same as Myles?

Jeanne   Younger. Myles was twenty-six on the fifth
of August. (*Pause.*) Major, did you just come here to

terrorise my child, or is there something I can do for you, before you leave?

Von Pfunz   Yes. You can help me with a problem I have.

Jeanne   What's that?

Von Pfunz   I am worried for you Jeanne, worried that you have a Jew sharing your home, eating the same food, spending time with your child . . .

Jeanne   Major –

Von Pfunz   She is a bad influence . . . this we can see. Why don't you throw her out?

Jeanne   She's my son's wife.

Von Pfunz   Why didn't she go back to England before the invasion? She must have known the danger.

Jeanne   She wanted to! I asked her to take Estelle to a cousin of mine in London. I knew I had to stay on the island; my house, you know, I wouldn't leave my house. Anyway, they got down to the harbour and everything was panic and mayhem. Estelle got frightened in the crowd and ran away. By the time Lilian found her, the last boat had sailed.

Von Pfunz   So it's the child's fault that the Jew is stranded here? Amazing, the damage innocence can cause . . . My problem: I have looked up her records and not only is she registered as a Christian, but her birthplace is given as Guernsey. I know this not to be true. Can you explain?

Jeanne   Major, I have to beg you not to continue this line of questioning.

Von Pfunz   I'm only looking for the truth.

Jeanne   Please, just leave things be.

Von Pfunz   Why must you protect her so? It's obvious you don't like her.

Jeanne   What I feel about her is not the point! I know I've got my faults but that kind of treachery isn't one of them. I couldn't live with myself.

Von Pfunz   Ah. A matter of conscience.

Jeanne   Yes.

Von Pfunz   The civilised person is capable of negotiating with conscience. One learns this in a war. Conscience will collaborate.

Jeanne   I've gone down that path as far as I intend.

Von Pfunz   But once you are on it, the path goes on forever. And you soon find you can live with anything. Jeanne, I have to report her.

Jeanne   Why?

Von Pfunz   All Jews must be registered.

Jeanne   What for?

Von Pfunz   Their own protection.

Pause. Jeanne shakily pours two drinks. She hands one to Von Pfunz.

Jeanne   What's your name Major? Your Christian name?

Von Pfunz   I have two; neither is relevant.

Jeanne   Well, Von Pfunz, I know you appreciate frank speech, so I'll speak frankly. I want to make a bargain with you.

Von Pfunz   What bargain?

Jeanne   I'll enter into any kind of relationship you might like, if you'll do one thing for me; leave my family alone.

Von Pfunz   Well! . . . (*He giggles.*) That's a very interesting offer, Jeanne.

Jeanne   Yes.

Von Pfunz   What can you mean by it?

Jeanne   Exactly what I said. Do you have a problem understanding?

Von Pfunz   You'll do anything I like, if I leave your family in peace?

Jeanne   Yes.

Von Pfunz   I'm overcome! (*He giggles.*) It's like Christmas and my birthday all at once . . . Jeanne Lascalles will do anything I want . . . (*Pause.*) Unfortunately, I can't think of anything.

> *Jeanne is lighting cigarettes, Hollywood style. She hands one to Von Pfunz.*

Jeanne   I'm being honest with you because I know you respect that. Don't lie to me. You can think of plenty.

Von Pfunz   You're right, of course. But forgive me Jeanne . . . I'm not sure that I like your bargain.

Jeanne   Why not?

Von Pfunz   Well, (*Giggles.*) it rather takes the spontaneity out of our relationship, don't you think? If I know that every moment you are with me is merely an act of martyrdom for your family? The more outrageous I was in my demands, the better you would feel. (*Laughing.*) Impossible! . . . Is this how you seduced Reicher?

Jeanne   Reicher was an attractive man. Are you? (*Pause.*) Do you think you'd stand the remotest chance with me, if I didn't have an ulterior motive?

Von Pfunz   Ah.

Jeanne Of course not. You know I find you repulsive; what's the point in lying?

Von Pfunz None ever.

Jeanne This is a way of keeping relations between us absolutely honest. You want me; I want to live without threat of harassment. Every 'prostitute' has a price and mine is peace of mind.

Pause. Von Pfunz is genuinely hurt and depressed.

Von Pfunz It's a sad picture of yourself you paint. You fling my insults back at me most cleverly, but the picture you paint is very sad . . .

Jeanne Perhaps you'd like some time to think over what I've said.

Von Pfunz Jeanne . . . Look how you tread yourself in the mud. It makes me so sad that your life has brought you to this. No wonder you have become bitter and desperate . . . To see your brightness squandered on this *tedious* struggle . . . sardines and Cognac – and your family like chains around your neck . . . You should be in Berlin, or Rome, or anywhere where there is *life*. You deserve to be alive. You are priceless.

Jeanne So, my bargain is a bargain then.

Von Pfunz Unfortunately, there's only one thing I want from you, and it's beyond your power to give.

Jeanne What is it?

Von Pfunz You can't imagine.

Jeanne I can imagine quite a lot.

Von Pfunz Jeanne . . . Sometimes our desires are so deep that we are not even sure of them ourselves. How can we ever be sure of what we really want? In speaking even our deepest desire aloud, it may become suddenly foolish, absurd on our lips, and no longer our desire . . .

Jeanne Are you worried that I would despise you?

Von Pfunz looks down.

Jeanne But . . . I despise you already. That shouldn't even be an issue.

Von Pfunz It isn't.

Jeanne Then ask for what you want.

Von Pfunz I can't.

Jeanne Why not?!

Von Pfunz (*sighs*) So. Your bargain is tempting but I must turn it down.

Jeanne No.

Jeanne kisses Von Pfunz. She holds her body close to his. Von Pfunz doesn't move or respond. After a moment, he lifts her away from him.

Von Pfunz Don't demean yourself, Mrs Becquet.

Von Pfunz goes to the door.

Von Pfunz Johann Sebastian.

Jeanne Ah.

Von Pfunz I'll call for you at nine o'clock. I think your nephew should come with us. A man of his education would be an invaluable guide, don't you think?

Jeanne I'm a good enough guide myself. I know the history of these islands better than anyone.

Von Pfunz Then you shall educate him. (*Pausing.*) Oxford . . . it's spires against a pearl grey sky. I dream of

one day walking through its streets; there must be wi
in the ground itself. Which college was he at?

Jeanne   Gabriel? Peterhouse.

   Von Pfunz takes a step back into the house.

Von Pfunz   You're very like your child, Jeanne. You
believe you're in no danger. You play with this war like a
game in your head.

Jeanne   What do you mean?

Von Pfunz   You think you are *inviolate* . . . Well, I have
some information for you; confidential.

Jeanne   Then keep it to yourself.

Von Pfunz   A launch of ours was lost at sea three nights
ago. One of the passengers was a young man, from Berlin.
When the wreck was found this morning, his body was
not in it.

Jeanne   How sad.

Von Pfunz   He was on his way to Alderney, to visit a new
camp there. It's run by the Schutzstaffel.

Jeanne   The who?

Von Pfunz   Hitler's brightest angels . . . the SS. This
young man was an officer.

Jeanne   Why are you telling me this?

Von Pfunz   No reason. He was quite an aristocrat,
apparently; educated at Oxford, like your nephew. He
spoke English like a native.

Jeanne   I'm sorry. I fail to see the relevance of this.

Von Pfunz   Perhaps there is none. I just want you to
be aware that penalties would be serious for hiding
information about him . . . if you had any. I fear for your

safety this evening Mrs Becquet, so I am posting a guard around the house.

Jeanne   Why on earth would you want to do that?

Von Pfunz   Because Peterhouse is a Cambridge college. I can't *believe* you don't know that. (*Sighs deeply.*) Jeanne . . . I give you time to come to terms with the truth. Anyone else I would have arrested already. Six armed men. I do this for you.

Von Pfunz goes. Jeanne locks and bolts the door. She sits. Her self-control crumbles.

Scene Four

The attic, later. Lamplight. Lily is sitting on the chair, mending a white shirt. Estelle is at the window, occasionally glancing out of it. Most of the time her attention is fixed on Gabriel, who is trying on a pair of cricket shoes.

Lily   Do they fit?

Gabriel   They're not bad. They're your husband's?

Lily   Yes.

Gabriel   I'm very grateful to him. (*He walks in them.*) Ja, schön . . .

Lily   Why you do that?

Gabriel   Do what?

Lily   Speak German. When you've forgotten everything else.

Gabriel   Well. My mind's not empty, if that's what you mean. It's full. (*Taking off the shoes.*) Of things, you know: facts – knowledge. German's so fluent I've been thinking in it. I know other languages too and music; I can hear phrases of it in my head. I haven't lost my knowledge – it's my whole experience that's gone. I don't remember a single thing that I've done or person that I've loved – nothing I can call mine. (*Pause.*) Except the falling.

Estelle   Falling?

Lily   He remembers falling.

Estelle   Out of the sky?

Gabriel   I don't know.

Lily   Try and think about the plane.

Gabriel   I don't remember a plane. (*Thinks.*) I can't see and I can't feel the wind; I'm neither warm nor cold but I'm falling fast . . . It's as if inside I'm hurtling downwards, while outside everything is still. I can't explain. It's more than just an image or a memory; it's a *thing* . . . consumes me.

Estelle   Is it frightening?

Gabriel   No. It's frightening when I look in the mirror and don't recognise the face. I'm a stranger to myself. What's left of me without the life I've lived?

Lily   Your own self. The essence of what you're like.

Gabriel   But I might as well have been born this afternoon.

Estelle   Gabriel –

Gabriel   Don't get me wrong; I'm not in despair. I'm fantastically glad to be alive. (*Pause.*) Everything feels new. That's the strangest thing. My senses are full. And this place . . . it's enchanting, isn't it?

Estelle nods and smiles. A beam of a torch light suddenly shines into the room from the yard below. It moves around and disappears. Estelle peers round the edge of the window.

Gabriel   What's that?

Lily   I expect Mrs Becquet's on her way to feed the hens. Here, try this on. I'll go and look.

Lily joins Estelle at the window. For a moment Gabriel briefly clutches his head.

Lily   (*quietly to Estelle*) Are they still there?

Estelle   It's hard to tell how many in the dark.

Lily   What are they doing?

Estelle   I don't know.

Lily   Searching the place or what?

Estelle   Just hanging around.

Lily   Go downstairs and ask your mum what's going on.

Estelle   We have to tell him. I know you said don't worry him with questions but he needs to know they're there, then he can think what to do.

Lily   What can he possibly do? . . .

Estelle   Lily, he has to prepare.

Gabriel   (*approaching*) Prepare for what?

Gabriel seems to be in some pain. He briefly holds his hand to his head.

Lily   Are you all right?

Gabriel   Fine. Who's out there?

Lily   No one.

Gabriel   Don't lie.

Estelle   There's some soldiers.

Gabriel   (*looking out of the window*) What soldiers?

Estelle   Krauts.

Gabriel   (*completely nonplussed*) . . . What do they want?

Estelle   Come away from the window; they might see you.

Gabriel   Why shouldn't they see me?

Estelle pulls Gabriel back into the room.

Gabriel   That man in your kitchen. They're the same, same uniform.

Lily   Yes.

Gabriel   Why are they here?

Lily   They're guarding the house.

Gabriel   What for?

Lily   You mustn't trouble yourself with it.

Estelle   He's got to trouble himself with it.

Gabriel   Are you connected with Germany in some way?

Lily   Pardon?

Gabriel   I mean, why are they German? We're in the middle of the English Channel. And their uniforms . . . ? The man in your kitchen, the same: eagles and the strange cross. I asked him what it was.

Lily   Oh.

Gabriel   He said I must have lived a very sheltered life. Of course, I couldn't argue with that – but what did he mean? (*Pause.*) What have I said?

Lily   You're in occupied Europe, Gabriel. Guernsey's occupied.

Gabriel   I don't understand.

Estelle   The Krauts have taken over the island. They bombed St Peter's Port and landed here in boats, thousands of them. They forced us out of our house and they're making us learn German in school. They march up and down all day and then at night they go to the pictures and watch films about Hitler. They've put barbed wire in the sea and planted mines on the beaches –

Gabriel   (*appalled*) Why?

Lily   Gabriel do you not remember *anything*? (*Pause.*) We're at war.

Gabriel looks utterly lost. He puts his hand to his head in increasing pain.

Lily   What's the matter?

Gabriel   But – wh – It's –

Lily   Is it your head? Gabriel, what is it? Here –

Gabriel   The Ger – we're the – the –

Lily   What is it?!

Gabriel suddenly cries out. He flings himself on to the bed.

Lily   Gabriel!

Estelle   What's wrong with him?

Gabriel cries out in agony.

Lily   I don't know!

Estelle   They'll hear him! They'll come inside! Put something over his mouth.

Lily   You'll smother him! Leave him.

Lily has to physically keep Estelle away from Gabriel.

Estelle   They'll take him away!

Lily   Give him space and *shut up*!

Estelle   *Gabriel!* . . .

*Gabriel passes out. Lily approaches him. She listens to
his chest etc. and tries to make him comfortable. Jeanne
enters unnoticed, with a glass of Cognac. She is drunk.*

Estelle Is he all right? . . .

Lily There must be something – . He must've injured his
head, when he fell. Estelle, I don't know . . . This happened
to him once before, when I was watching him. The way
he cried out. The pain, here. I thought it was the fever . . .
some kind of pressure building up. Maybe that's all it is . . .

Estelle (*climbing on to the bed*) He'll be better now.
Won't he.

Gabriel slowly comes round.

Gabriel Lily . . .

Lily How are you?

Gabriel I was falling.

Lily Like before?

Gabriel nods.

Lily Nothing else?

Gabriel It takes hold of me.

Lily How?

Gabriel The speed . . . hurts.

Estelle You mustn't do it again.

Gabriel No. No . . .

Lily Rest.

Gabriel (*pause*) There's another image.

Lily What?

Gabriel Snow.

Lily   Snow?

Gabriel   I'm standing in snow. Everything white . . . And the dead sound things make when it's deep. Something behind me . . . like a fear. I'm wearing black.

Jeanne   Estelle, get off there.

Estelle   (*staring with shock*) I'm cold.

Jeanne   Get off.

Lily   Mrs Becquet . . . Fancy you hiding there.

Estelle reluctantly gets off Gabriel's bed.

Jeanne   Wie geht es dir, meine kleine deutsche Junge? (*How are you, little German boy?*)

Gabriel   Danke, gut; es geht mir gut. (*Fine thank you; I'm fine.*)

Jeanne   Do you know who I am?

Gabriel   Mrs Becquet.

Jeanne   And who are you?

Lily   He doesn't know.

Jeanne   I asked him, not you. Who *are* you?

Gabriel   I've been given the name Gabriel. I was born this afternoon.

Jeanne   Well Gabriel, I never wanted another child in my house.

Gabriel   By that, I mean I don't know who I am. I'm sorry.

Jeanne   Why be sorry? No one's blaming you for anything, are they?

Gabriel   No.

Jeanne   So. Have you had plenty to eat and drink?

Gabriel   Yes, thank you.

Jeanne   I see Lilian's giving you my son's favourite clothes.

Lily   His cricket things.

Jeanne   That's right.

Lily   It's all he left behind.

Estelle   Daddy's clothes are too small.

Lily   And he's got to wear something, hasn't he?

Jeanne   She found you naked, did you know that?

Gabriel   Yes.

Jeanne   It's a shame really because if you'd been clothed, we'd've known who you were, straight away. We only had your features to judge you by and they can be so misleading, don't you think?

Gabriel   I'm sure.

Jeanne   So . . . you wear black in your dreams. (*To Lily.*) Does he know the danger he's put us in?

Lily   It's not his fault.

Gabriel   What have I done?

Lily   Nothing.

Jeanne   You'd be dead if it wasn't for me and my family. We put our lives at risk to help you. I've kept you in this house against my will for three days.

Lily   You said he could stay!

Jeanne   I didn't say he could betray us.

Lily   He hasn't.

Gabriel What have I done?

Jeanne You know damn well.

Lily It's not his fault! He didn't know who the Major was. He can't remember the war.

Jeanne He *what*?

Lily He can't remember the war.

Jeanne Don't be absurd!

Gabriel What war?

Jeanne Of course he can remember the bloody war!

Gabriel What war? I need to know.

Jeanne What kind of a game are you playing?

Lily Leave him alone Mrs Becquet; you'll make him ill again!

Jeanne This is *my house!* Don't you tell me what I can and can't do!

Lily retreats, defeated.

Jeanne You don't know anything about the war?

Gabriel shakes his head.

Jeanne Well. I have to say, I don't believe you. I have to say, I don't trust you an inch. So, without going into too much detail, the whole world has been at war for the last three years; that's everybody, everywhere. Ring any bells? Unless you've been living in a hermit's cave in the Antarctic, you really can't have missed it . . . In Europe, the baddies are Nazis. They're German, they wear grey, and they want to rule the world. We're with the Allies, who wear green.

Gabriel So, the man I met –

Jeanne Is our enemy, yes. And tomorrow, because he's discovered we're hiding you, and because hiding you is a Very Serious Crime, he's going to come here like a cat tormenting mice. He'll spend the day playing with us and afterwards, he'll arrest my family and me. Then, when we've all been *raped* by him –

Lily Enough! –

Jeanne He'll have us shot.

Gabriel (*despairing*) I didn't know . . .

Jeanne There was a German soldier in my kitchen, walking around with a gun on his belt. Did you think he was in fancy dress?

Estelle We fooled him, Gabriel. He thinks you're my cousin. We told him your name's Gabriel Lascalles and you come from Torteval. You work on Uncle Maurice's vegetable farm and you went to Oxford but the war's sadly clipped your wings . . .

The torch light shines into the room again. Jeanne goes to the window. She looks into the light. She raises her glass, then drinks. Pause. The light disappears.

Gabriel What do you want me to do, Mrs Becquet?

Jeanne Our punishment, Liebling, will depend on who you are. Some fugitives are more sacred than others, and perhaps you're only a stupid island drunkard who hit his head on a rock. You have to remember.

Gabriel I can't.

Jeanne Then they'll assume what they like. Are you a British pilot, Gabriel, like my son?

Gabriel I don't know.

Jeanne Or are you German? You speak it so damn well.

Do you think you're English just because you heard it first, when you woke up?

Estelle   He can speak lots of languages. He hears them in his head. He's got infinite knowledge, Mummy, but no experience. That's why he can't think of –

Jeanne   Estelle, if I hear one more word out of you I'm going to thrash you into bed! (*To Gabriel.*) The fact is, the Major knows who you are.

Gabriel   How?

Jeanne   He says you're a shining SS officer who was washed off a boat on his way to Alderney.

Lily   No.

Jeanne   Do you know what they are, the SS?

Gabriel shakes his head.

Jeanne   They're the élite; Germany's hand-picked men; brave, proud, wonderfully handsome. Lilian especially lives in terror of them.

Gabriel   Why?

Lily   (*to Jeanne*) Shut up!

Jeanne   They're the most transcendent men on Earth, the first citizens of the new world. Sadly, their new world only seems achievable by destroying the old. They regard most of us as sub-human and the Jews, whom they hate, as a plague.

Lily   You're unbelievably drunk.

Jeanne   They wear black, shining, lacquered black. It'd suit you so well, don't you think? . . .

Lily   This is nonsense!

Jeanne   Because you don't want it to be true? I'm very sorry Lilian. Believe me, I am. But this one of Hitler's brightest angels; one of his chosen few. Darkness visible.

Estelle   You've made a mistake . . .

Jeanne   Estelle, I have not. There's a concentration camp on Alderney that you were on your way to visit. Alderney's a secret place these days. Half the troops don't know what goes on . . . But we hear things. It's full of slaves; emaciated wrecks worked to death and their corpses thrown into –

Estelle   (*screeching, hands over ears*) Stop it Mummy!

Jeanne   I'm sorry darling. It's too horrible for words, isn't it? (*To Gabriel.*) Is it true that you can't remember anything about yourself or the war?

Gabriel   Yes it's true.

Jeanne   Then what made you blank it out? What have you done that you can't live with? Was it all too much to bear? All the blood on your hands . . . You could be this man, couldn't you? It's possible.

Gabriel   Ja, möglich ist es. Alles ist möglich. (*Yes, it's possible. Anything is possible . . .*)

Jeanne   I've had nightmares since you came here. Every night, since they dragged you in . . . (*Voice cracking.*) You look like my son.

Lily   He does *not!* . . .

Jeanne   Do you hear me?

Gabriel   Yes.

Jeanne   You look like Myles, my son.

Gabriel   I can't help that.

Jeanne   He's dead isn't he? My son is dead . . .

Estelle   No! . . .

Jeanne   That's the truth . . . (*Screeches.*) I can *feel* it! . . .

Jeanne sobs. She drops her empty glass. The torch light shines into the room again. It moves around and disappears. Only Lily and Gabriel notice. They look at one another.

Estelle   Mummy . . . don't cry. It's not true . . .

Estelle touches Jeanne, who flinches, stands and stumbles towards the door.

Jeanne   Ohh . . . God . . .

Lily   What now?

Jeanne   Going to be sick.

Lily grips Jeanne by the arm.

Lily   Downstairs. Now. I'll get you a bucket.

Lily leads Jeanne out roughly. Pause. Estelle gets on the bed beside Gabriel.

Estelle   Myles isn't dead. I'd feel it too, if he was. He isn't dead, I know it. Mummy's wrong. She's wrong about everything. I know you're not that man.

Gabriel kisses the crown of Estelle's head.

Estelle   You came for me didn't you? . . .

Gabriel   What do you mean?

Estelle   The night you came, I made a square of power. Everything that's happened has come out of it. It's the most powerful shape there is. You draw it in chalk and make the secret signs and then you wish.

Gabriel   Oh.

Estelle At first I thought it wasn't going to work but Lily must've found you at the exact moment, the exact moment when I made my wish.

Gabriel What was your wish?

Estelle I went with her down to the beach to help her bring you back. And when I saw you lying there in the sand, I knew that when I'd said, let my brother come like a bright angel, what I'd really meant was, let a bright angel come like my brother . . .

Gabriel (*pause*) Estelle.

Estelle I know why you can't tell anyone who you are. It's because they'd never believe you. It was my square of power again, that saved your life. I made sure we laid you right on top of it and you survived. You took the power and it went right through you. And I still didn't know it was you, but I was hoping, hoping all the time. And all you can remember is falling . . . You remember falling and everything is new to you –

Gabriel Look –

Estelle (*hugging him*) I love you Gabriel I love you and I want you to know that I've already started to help. I decided the night you came and I've been braver than ever in my life. I smashed his Hitler and wee'd in his boot, and I stole his book to read his secrets and destroy his plans – and even when I was *so* frightened I didn't give you away, even when he said those *horrible* things to me . . . and none of them are true, none of them! I'm *not* the one that nobody likes! –

Gabriel Estelle – Look –

Estelle I know I'm good because *you* love me! . . . And I know it's hard because you've fallen so far and it's hurt you so much but even Mrs Lake said if you survived it'd be a miracle and you have Gabriel, you have! –

Gabriel All right –

Estelle When the time comes . . . I'll help you. He's spreading lies about you because he can see that you're pure and good. He told me what Force was, Gabriel, and I knew he meant Evil; all the while I was looking at him thinking Evil, Evil, Evil.

Gabriel   . . . Estelle, what is it you think I can do?

Estelle   (*simply*) You've come to crush and destroy them. You've got to kill Major Von Pfunz.

Lily comes in, with Von Pfunz's diary hidden under her cardigan.

Lily Come on. Time for bed.

Estelle Where's Mummy?

Lily In the chair by the fire.

Estelle Was she sick?

Lily She'd eaten some biscuits that had gone off.

Estelle Can I go and see if she's better?

Lily She's asleep. Go to bed.

Estelle Is that the Major's book?

Lily Yes.

Estelle (*to Gabriel*) It's the one I told you about. He said it was just full of poems – but if it is, why does he care so much about getting it back? (*Whispers.*) I love you.

Estelle kisses Gabriel and gets out of his bed. She kisses Lily and exits. Lily puts Von Pfunz's book on the bed.

Gabriel What is it?

Lily Estelle stole it off the Major. I thought if you could speak German you could probably read it too and you might find something that . . . will help you.

Gabriel   Help me do what?

Lily   Remember.

Gabriel   I see. Is that wise?

Lily   (*pause*) Gabriel . . .

Gabriel   I'm only sure of one thing, Lily. Gabriel is not my name. (*Gabriel gets up. Sighs.*) I'm lost in every way . . . The things in my mind make no sense. First I'm told I'm a pilot – and then – (*Pause.*) What do you think?

Lily   About what?

Gabriel   About me. Who do you believe I am?

Lily   I believe the same as you.

Gabriel   And what's that?

Lily   That you don't know.

> *Gabriel looks despairing. Lily goes to him and puts a hand on his shoulder. Gabriel hugs her. She comforts him. Gabriel stands, still in the embrace. They look at one another. They kiss. It's becoming very passionate when Lily breaks away.*

Lily   NO! I can't . . .

Gabriel   I'm sorry . . . (*Pause.*) Your husband –

Lily   No. It's not to do with Myles. I don't love him. When we got married I thought I did, but it was false. It was false and I got stuck here. I want to tell you something else.

Gabriel   What?

Lily   (*looking straight at him*) I'm a Jew.

Gabriel   . . . What should that mean to me?

Lily   You tell me. What should it mean?

Gabriel Do you . . . is it that you have a religious objection to – to us being –

Lily (*half laugh, half sob*).

Gabriel (*remembering*) No. Those people hate you.

Lily (*near to tears*) The Jews on this island have gone . . . No one knows where. I knew two women. Police came, handed them to the Krauts, never seen again. The only reason I'm still here is cause Mrs Becquet protects me. We hear rumours about things in Europe. God help me . . . (*They embrace.*)

Gabriel Why have you told me?

Lily I thought, if you were one of them I'd be able to tell.

Gabriel Can you?

  Lily shakes her head.

Gabriel Lily, I'm lost, so lost. Don't turn against me –

Lily I'm not. I just need to know you won't turn against me . . .

  They kiss passionately. They go to the bed.

Lily Who are you?

  The torch light shines in.

Gabriel (*he kisses her*) This. (*Kisses her again.*) I'm this . . .

Scene Five

The kitchen. Moonlight. Jeanne is asleep in the chair by the fire, a blanket over her knees. She looks awful.

Estelle enters, wearing her night dress. She is holding a candle. She looks at her mother. She goes to a drawer in the dresser and takes out something wrapped in a red cloth. She puts the candle and the cloth bundle on the floor. She draws a chalk square. She kneels in it and makes her secret signs, as previously. She unwraps the bundle. Inside it is an old First World War dagger. She examines it. She holds it up by the tip and slowly lays it in the square. She stands back, her eyes fixed on the dagger.

Pause.

Jeanne snores. Estelle looks at her once more and exits with the candle.

The attic. Lily is asleep. Gabriel is staring into space. He looks at Lily. He touches her.

He goes to the window and peers out. He sees Von Pfunz's book lying on the floor. He picks it up. He flicks through it. He sits on the bed and starts reading.

Scene Six

Dawn. The kitchen. Jeanne is awake, but unmoving. She leans forward and sighs. Someone knocks loudly on the back door. Jeanne starts. She stands and leans dizzily against the table. She attempts to neaten her appearance, panicked and ill.

Jeanne   (*calls*) Just a minute! (*More knocking. She fumbles across the room.*) . . . Would you wait a moment please?

Lake   (*off*) It's me.

Jeanne   Margaret . . .

Lake   (*knocking*) Come on, let me in.

Jeanne   Wait.

   Jeanne unlocks the door. Lake enters.

Lake   Bloody little bleeders wouldn't let me by. What's been going on up here?

Jeanne   I thought you were him.

Lake   Who?

Jeanne   Him.

   Jeanne flops back into her chair and closes her eyes.

Lake   What's going on, Jean? Why are those lads out there?

Jeanne   Margaret, I desperately need a cup of tea . . .

Lake   Marvellous.

Lake puts fuel in the stove and puts the kettle on the hob. Jeanne raises her head.

Jeanne   Where have you been?

Lake   Where you sent me. I walked up here last night, found it covered in Krauts. One of them's a lad I know so I says to him: 'Come on, I live here, you have to let me through,' but he wouldn't – didn't even tell me what was going on.

Jeanne   Where did you go?

Lake   Pub. Slept in the lounge. Mrs Garrett gave me a blanket. What have you done to yourself, Jean?

Jeanne   I just had a couple of drinks.

Lake   Then you don't need tea.

Lake cracks a raw egg into a cup. She pours in some milk, adds two spoons of sugar and whisks it with a fork.

Jeanne   Not one of those . . .

Lake   Why are the lads out there?

Jeanne   The Major saw the boy.

Lake   He saw the boy? . . .

Jeanne   It was love at first sight. The boy started chatting in fluent German and now Von Pfunz is convinced he's some missing Nazi.

Lake   He speaks German?

Jeanne nods.

Lake   Does he still not remember himself?

Jeanne shakes her head.

Lake   What's the Major going to do?

Jeanne   I don't know . . .

Lake   (*handing her the drink*) Drink.

Jeanne   (*she drinks. She pulls a face*) Ugh! . . . May the ground open and swallow me.

Lake   It was a mistake to take that boy in, Jean.

Jeanne   I knew that!

Lake   It would have been kinder to let him die.

Jeanne   Why? . . . What have you found out?

Lake   The truth.

Lily enters.

Jeanne   Lilian.

Lily   How are you, Mrs Becquet? . . .

Jeanne   I never felt better, thank you. How are you?

Lily   I think you should see this.

Lily puts Von Pfunz's diary in front of Jeanne. Jeanne picks it up.

Jeanne   What is it?

Lily   The Major's book.

Jeanne   The Major's book . . . Where did you find it?

Lily   Estelle gave it to me.

Jeanne   I might have known . . . (*Flicking through it.*) Damn, it's in German.

Lily   Gabriel read it during the night.

Jeanne   What's in it?

Lily   Stuff about Poland. Things he's seen there.

Jeanne   What things?

Lily   (*sits*) They're killing Jews. In these huge places like factories. Shipping trainloads of people into Poland and gassing them.

Jeanne   What?

Lily   He describes it in detail, the whole . . . process. It's on a scale you can't imagine.

Jeanne   Nonsense.

Lily   I never read anything that made me sick before. Gabriel woke me in the night. He said I ought to hear. It's the truth.

Lake   But Europe's crawlin' with Jews. They couldn't kill 'em all if they had fifty years . . .

Jeanne   It's nonsense. Lilian – there must be something in here we can use, something that makes him weak, information we can use against him.

Lily   I never thanked you much for sticking your neck out over me, Mrs Becquet. But I'm truly grateful.

   Lily suppresses tears.

Jeanne   Lily . . . (*She hesitates.*) This is simply not true. Von Pfunz is a very sick man and he's making it up. We're talking about civilised Europe! This is the twentieth century, not the Middle Ages. Now please, calm yourself and tell me if there's anything in that book that we can hold over him, anything that damns him, in any way.

Lily   The whole thing damns him.

   Gabriel enters, dressed in cricketing gear.

Gabriel   Good morning.

Jeanne   Good morning. How are you?

Gabriel   Fine, thank you. (*To Lake, holding out his hand.*) I don't believe we've met . . .

Lily   This is Lake.

Lake   (*awkwardly shaking his hand*) I brought you through your fever.

Gabriel   Then I must thank you too, for saving my life.

Lake   I didn't.

Jeanne   Gabriel, I want to know about this book. I want to know what Von Pfunz says about himself. There must be something in here we can use.

Lily   She doesn't believe me.

Gabriel   Oh.

Lily   Would you read her something? Then she'll believe it.

Jeanne   I'm sorry but we haven't got time.

Gabriel   Which one?

Lily   The room full of hair.

Gabriel   I'll translate it for you. (*Reads title in German then translates.*) 'Abgegeben . . . ', 'Discarded . . . ':

> Like a field of corn or the sea
> hair heaped to the rafters
> high as hay.
> The secret in this place
> is loud in the sunlight
> dark in the silence
> like a brown curl it clings.
> I tear it from me.

Jeanne What does it mean?

Gabriel What it says. He's seen a room filled with hair. He's written almost everything in poetic form so it takes a while for the – *darkness* of it to reach your heart . . .

Lily Read another.

Gabriel (*reads the title in German, then translates*) 'Die Unerwählten . . . ', 'The Unselected . . . ':

> The Selector loves the dark, the mask
> And cloak it throws around his task.
> These shadowed wraiths,
> Pouring out of wagon gates
> A shambles of limbs unsteady,
> Are creatures half born
> To the spirit world already.
>
> Survive or be damned.
> They pass
> Where the Selector stands
> And it is done.
> A firmament of human eyes
> Stare into the shadows that are his
> Yet he is calm at source.
> For the Selector does not choose;
> His hand moves left and right
> An independent thing, a tool
> Not of his but of the rule
> That thralls us – Force.
>
> The Unselected learn their fate
> Too late to curse him to his face,
> Nor does he care to feel
> Their soon annihilated hate.
> The Selector cloaked
> In darkness stands
> As judges must
> When judgement is at hand.

Pause.

Lily   (*to Gabriel*) Read the one about the child's shoe.

Jeanne   I've heard enough.

Lily   It's lying in the snow. He bends down to pick it up and he finds the frozen child underneath. He calls it a pearl of great price.

Gabriel   Ein wahrer Schatz. (*A pearl of great price.*)

Jeanne   Lilian . . .

Gabriel   What shall we do?

Jeanne   Nothing.

Gabriel   Nothing?

Jeanne   I'm sorry, (*Takes it from him.*) but he mustn't know that you've read it. Lily, take it up to Estelle and dress her in something clean. (*Pause.*) I don't want any harm to come to my daughter. She has to give it back.

Gabriel puts a hand to his head as if he's in pain.

Lily   What's the matter?

Gabriel   Nothing.

Lily   Are you all right?

Gabriel nods.

Lily   Are you sure? Gabriel . . . (*She touches him.*)

Gabriel   (*the pain seems to have passed*) Yes.

Lily realises her gesture has compromised her. Jeanne and Lake are both looking at her.

Lily   I'll wake Estelle.

She exits upstairs with the book.

Lake I must tell you something, boy.

Gabriel What?

Lake There's no easy way to say it so I'll just say it. I heard this story last night from Mrs Garrett, a landlady who's got ears everywhere. She got it from a woman in St Peter's Port; one of your wife's people.

Jeanne You know who he is.

Lake Your name ain't Gabriel, it's John Gilbert. You work in a bank, translating for the Krauts.

Gabriel I what?

Lake You been missing a couple of weeks and your family all feared you was dead.

Jeanne What makes you think this is him? It could be anyone.

Lake I asked Mrs Garrett what sort of young man it was and she said uncommon good-looking, like some painting out of church and that's him.

Gabriel (*slight laugh*)

Lake This winter, you start getting this bad vision and pains in your eyes and they turn into these like fits, and no one knows what's wrong with you so they take you to the Kraut doctors and the Kraut doctors do all manner of tests and that, and then one of them takes you aside and says there's a thing growing in your head that ain't right, something growing in there and they're sorry but there's nothing they can do.

Jeanne My God . . .

Lake You go to pieces after that and run off. Then, the same day as Lilian finds you, three men see you over where they're building the tunnels, no shoes on, all besmirched and cut up on your legs. They reckon you been hiding down there. Last they see, you was running off to the beach, stumbling like you're blinded in the light.

Jeanne This is unbelievable . . .

Lake I'm sorry my boy, but I thought you ought to know.

Jeanne Margaret, do you know what this means? . . . We can't be prosecuted for hiding him if he's only an island man. If he's sick, what crime have we committed by having him here?

Lake None.

Jeanne That's right, none . . . (*To Gabriel.*) I'm so sorry . . . This is awful news for you; truly tragic, but at the risk of sounding callous, I have to say that it's very good news for us.

Gabriel Yes.

Jeanne It's one thing less, one thing less . . . Margaret, come and help me with my hair.

Jeanne exits to her room.

Lake I'm sorry.

Gabriel Nothing you've said makes the slightest connection with me. It's just as foreign and just as possible as anything else I've heard. John Gilbert. Blinded in the light.

Lake Well. Like I say, I'm sorry.

Gabriel There is one thing.

Lake What?

Gabriel I can see perfectly.

*Lake exits to Jeanne's room. Gabriel has another spasm
of pain.*

Gabriel Oh, hilf mir, hilf mir. Wer bin ich? (*Oh, help me,
help me. Who am I?*)

*Gabriel's eyes suddenly alight on the dagger in the
chalk square. He looks at it, puzzled. He picks it up.
He stands in the square and examines it. He realises
where he is standing. He kneels. Pause. He suddenly
puts his ear to the ground, as if he has heard something
below. Estelle enters from the stairs, neatly dressed, her
hair loose. She approaches Gabriel.*

Estelle Can you hear them?

Gabriel (*starting with shock*) Who?

Estelle The men underneath. They're coming right under
the house.

Gabriel You've got men underneath?

Estelle Yes.

Gabriel What are they doing?

Estelle Making a labyrinth for the Krauts. Will you
make them stop?

Gabriel (*pause*) What's this Estelle?

He holds up the knife. Estelle takes it.

Estelle A knife. It's been gathering power.

Gabriel Right . . .

Estelle I wanted to get you a gun but the Krauts keep
them all locked up. Daddy had one, a revolver, but he
buried it after the Great War and no one knows where.
He had this in the trenches. Mummy says he used it for
killing rats but I think it was Krauts. (*She hands it back
to Gabriel.*) Will it do?

Gabriel   For what?

Estelle   For him. You just have to find your chance . . . (*Pause*.) I'll help all I can.

Gabriel   (*goes to the armchair*) Estelle . . . I don't need this.

Estelle   Why not?

Gabriel   (*smiles, ironically*) I'm going to smite him with a thunderbolt.

> *Estelle giggles. The door bursts open and Von Pfunz enters, carrying a jackboot. Gabriel is hidden from his view by the chair. He puts the dagger in his belt behind him.*

Von Pfunz   Where is your mother?

Estelle   (*backing away*) It's rude to come in without knocking.

Von Pfunz   I want her now!

Estelle   Why?

Von Pfunz   You know why! (*Holding up the jackboot.*) Explain!

> *Estelle looks afraid and ashamed.*

Von Pfunz   Next time you come near my house I will tell my men to shoot!

Estelle   (*looking at the floor*) It's *my* house . . .

Von Pfunz   That a little girl could do this! It sickens me. You are like an *animal*, a filthy dirty –

Gabriel   (*stands*) Guten Morgen, Herr Major. (*Good morning, Major.*)

Von Pfunz   Herr Lascalles. Versteckt hat sie sich, in meinem Haus . . . (*Mr Lascalles. She's been hiding in my house . . .*)

Gabriel (*smiling*) Ich weiß; und schikaniert hat sie Sie auch noch, die Kleine. (*So I gather; terrorising you single-handedly.*)

Von Pfunz Ein Verbrechen hat sie begangen. (*She has perpetrated a crime.*)

Gabriel What's she done?

Von Pfunz It is almost too shameful to say. She has urinated in my boot.

Lily enters, dressed up. She stares at Von Pfunz. Estelle runs to her.

Von Pfunz Mrs Myles. Good morning.

Lily I have to brush her hair.

Lily exits with Estelle.

Von Pfunz These are my finest boots. The best in Munich. I was to wear them for my day with Mrs Becquet. You can imagine my disgust. (*He puts his boot down. Pause.*) Your flu is better?

Gabriel Yes, thank you.

Von Pfunz You have good rest last night?

Gabriel Not really. I couldn't sleep.

Von Pfunz I sent my men to watch over you.

Gabriel It wasn't your men that kept me awake. I was reading.

Von Pfunz Good book?

Gabriel Poetry.

Von Pfunz Ah . . . You are a lover of poetry?

Gabriel It fascinates me.

Von Pfunz The treasure of England.

Gabriel Yes.

Von Pfunz I grew up with Keats and Donne. (*Giggles.*) I dabble a little myself . . .

Gabriel You write poetry?

Von Pfunz Yes. I am hoping one day to be published.

Gabriel Oh . . .

Von Pfunz You find it unusual for a soldier to write?

Gabriel A little, yes.

Von Pfunz But poetry is a voice of truth, and truth is revealed most clearly in extremities. Soldiers live in extremities; they are in the mouth of death.

Gabriel But surely not all soldiers see the truth, even when they're staring right at it.

Von Pfunz I quite agree. It is the soul of a poet that sees the truth, but sometimes such a soul is trapped in a soldier's life. It is the soul of a poet that can unravel the chaos he is in and make it something pure. You see, the poet believes that only when we struggle to understand on a greater scale, do we know that we're alive, that we're more than a machine . . . The poet sees the greater truth. (*Pause.*) I think you are fooling me. You know all this; you were at Oxford!

Gabriel But I don't remember ever speaking to a living poet. What do you mean by the greater truth?

Von Pfunz (*giggles*) You ask me this before breakfast? (*Thinks.*) I mean an honesty so pure it hurts us. A superior state, of light, where all is clear. Such a thing is possible only as a dream – but the search is poetry. To choose the face of truth hardest to look into. That is where one finds something pure.

Gabriel   I see.

Von Pfunz   I think for most of us it's a moment that comes only with death.

Gabriel   You see death as a greater truth?

Von Pfunz   As a kind of purity, yes. It's rather a cliché, I know.

Gabriel   So purity can be absolute darkness as well as absolute light?

Von Pfunz   Yes . . .

Gabriel   How would you define evil?

Von Pfunz   (*giggles, delighted*) You are playing in a cricket match today?

Gabriel   No. These are my clothes.

Jeanne enters hurriedly, dressed for a day out. Lake follows her.

Jeanne   Major, I thought I could hear your voice. Forgive me for keeping you. I was just putting the finishing touches to my hair. (*Noticing the boot.*) What's that?

Von Pfunz   That is my boot.

Jeanne   What's it doing in my kitchen?

Von Pfunz   It is the victim of an outrage.

Jeanne   I'm sorry?

Von Pfunz   Your daughter has emptied her bladder here.

Jeanne   She's done nothing of the kind!

Von Pfunz   You can see for yourself.

Von Pfunz takes the boot to the sink. He empties it.

Von Pfunz That is the evidence. These are waterproof and I put my foot right in. I was revolted.

Jeanne My daughter is a young lady . . . How dare you.

Von Pfunz I demand that it is cleaned.

Jeanne One of your pig soldiers did it. Make them clean it!

Von Pfunz Madam, this has gone far enough. Your child will clean this while I watch!

Jeanne Over my dead body.

Von Pfunz I am lenient with her because she is your child but I have had the limit! She will clean this boot or I am telling my men to shoot all trespassers – and we shall see then if she can haunt us!

Jeanne (*appalled*) Are you threatening her life?

Von Pfunz I am saying I have had enough!

Jeanne (*livid*) You should remember where you are. This island is a civilised place. You may be in the habit of shooting children – but let me tell you, soldiers have been court-martialled here for your kind of sick bullying. I'm fed up with you and your repulsive threats. I take full responsibility for Estelle, so why don't you arrest me? Why don't you arrest all of us right now?

Von Pfunz Jeanne . . . this is not –

Jeanne Take whoever you're going to take, and get out! You're dis*gu*sting . . .

Von Pfunz (*shocked*) It was a figure of speech you know, words I use all the time: I say all the time, 'Do this or that or I will have you shot'; these are not words I mean! I would not harm you child! . . . You must forgive my

mistakes, my – . It is language problems . . . Mrs Becquet,
we must go to the ruins. I have ordered a picnic . . .

Jeanne Am I under arrest?

Von Pfunz No.

Jeanne Is anyone else here under arrest?

Von Pfunz This is mistaken –

Jeanne Then *get out!*

  Pause. Von Pfunz exits.

Jeanne What have I done? I meant to appease him . . .
Oh God, I've buggered it up . . .

Lake (*looking out of the window*) He's doing something.

Jeanne He's lining up a bloody firing squad. God!

Lake No, he's talking to them. I don't know what he's
doing.

Jeanne What have I done?

Gabriel Mrs Becquet, I was talking to him about the
greater truth.

Jeanne I beg your pardon?

Gabriel The greater truth. I think he's a soul sunk into
darkness.

Jeanne Thank you, I'll remember that useful fact.

Lake They're going! Look, he's told them to go!

Jeanne Why?

Lake I don't know, do I?

Gabriel In his book, there's a poem about you.

Jeanne What poem?

Gabriel He says you see him for what he is. He says you're –

Lake He's coming back. I'll lock him out!

Jeanne No! (*To Gabriel.*) What?

Gabriel Großartig.

Jeanne (*irritated*) Well, that's marvellous.

Von Pfunz knocks on the door.

Gabriel It means magnificent.

Jeanne (*to Lake*) Open it.

Lake opens the door.

Von Pfunz May I speak with Mrs Becquet please?

Jeanne (*to Lake*) Ask him the purpose of his call.

Von Pfunz Yes, Mrs Becquet I have sent my men away. I wish to – . They are not needed here now but you must let me in.

Jeanne Would you ask the Major to come in?

Lake stands back. Von Pfunz enters.

Von Pfunz I know why the child hates me. It is your house I live in, your island I occupy . . . I am the enemy. Of course she hates me for all these things. I forget, you see, what it is like for her. Things have different meanings to a child. They do not see the same. And really, I like her. She is brave and – . I feel bad about so many things! . . . Jeanne, I have sent my men away. I am not – I am not . . . disgusting.

Jeanne Major.

Von Pfunz I am a slave of Force. This must be. If I were my own master . . . I would never be hated by children. It *pains* me. I long to be her friend!

Jeanne   (*pause*) Would you like a cup of tea?

Von Pfunz   Thank you.

Jeanne   Margaret, perhaps you'd make a pot. Please . . . sit down.

Von Pfunz   Thank you.

Von Pfunz sits. Lake starts making tea.

Jeanne   Well, this is more civilised isn't it, Johann? Unpleasantness before breakfast can spoil the whole day.

Von Pfunz   I look forward greatly to our trip. The ruins.

Jeanne   I thought we'd start at La Catioroc, a great stone like an altar. It looks over the beach, nearby. The devil was supposed to stand on it to call his demons out of the sea. They're building gun placements there. Have you breakfasted?

Von Pfunz   After discovering my boot, I lost interest in my poached eggs.

Jeanne   A tragedy . . . Please, let me feed you. Margaret, what do we have?

Lake   Bread and jam.

Jeanne   Gabriel dear, would you put that thing outside? It's so unsightly.

Gabriel puts the boot outside. Lake is cutting and buttering bread.

Jeanne   The English Channel was a forest when the first people came here. Some days, when the tide is low, you can still see the stumps of carbonised trees.

Von Pfunz   Fan*tas*tic . . . One could believe the history of all Europe starts here. (*Confidentially.*) There's something however that we must discuss first, something I cannot leave. This is hard but I must do my duty. Your daughter-in-law.

Jeanne What about her?

Von Pfunz You would like to see her live somewhere else, yes?

Jeanne No! You know I wouldn't –

Von Pfunz These things are hard to admit, even to yourself. She must register her real identity and then I can move her for you.

Jeanne No!

Estelle and Lily enter. Estelle carries Von Pfunz's book.

Von Pfunz Here she comes. Look how she clings to the child. This is the bad influence.

Lily Major. Estelle wants to say something to you.

Von Pfunz Well.

Estelle I'm sorry for taking your book.

Estelle puts the book on the table. Lily sits.

Lily Estelle and I share a room. I found it under her pillow this morning, when I was making her bed. I thought it could only be yours.

Von Pfunz Thank you. (*He picks up the book, as if reunited with something precious.*) It would have been terrible to lose it. (*He pockets it.*)

Jeanne (*to Estelle*) You lied to me and you lied to the Major. What have you got to say for yourself?

Estelle Nothing.

Von Pfunz Why did you steal it?

Estelle   I wanted to give it to someone.

Von Pfunz   Who?

Estelle   The Resistance.

Von Pfunz   The Resistance! . . . And how did you propose to get it to them?

Estelle   Don't know.

Jeanne   She reads too many adventure books.

Von Pfunz   Estelle, I'm sad to tell you, that alone of all the occupations I have partaken in, Guernsey has no Resistance. Nothing organised, that we can find. It's what makes it so pleasant to stay here. There is no troupe of brave young men hiding in the hills, because there are no brave young men and no hills! (*He giggles.*) Now. What am I to do with you? (*Giggling.*) I think perhaps, if I were to lock you in the tunnels, you would know what it was to feel haunted.

Lake   (*slams a plate of bread and jam down in front of Von Pfunz*) Breakfast.

Von Pfunz   . . . Estelle, shake my hand. I am determined we shall be friends.

Estelle shakes Von Pfunz's hand.

Von Pfunz   Now, give me a kiss.

Estelle hesitates.

Jeanne   Kiss him, darling, he's being nice.

Estelle reluctantly kisses Von Pfunz. He pulls her onto his knee.

Von Pfunz   There! How is that?

Estelle   Mummy . . .

Jeanne   Make friends!

Von Pfunz   You must help me eat all this bread and jam! . . . (*To Gabriel.*) I hope our trip today will take us as far as Torteval, Mr Lascalles.

Gabriel   Why?

Von Pfunz   I'm longing to meet your family.

Gabriel   Me too. I can't imagine what they're like.

Von Pfunz   (*taken aback*) What do you mean?

Jeanne   Sebastian . . . I have a confession to make.

Gabriel   Mrs Becquet hat mir Schutz geboten. (*Mrs Becquet has been protecting me.*)

Von Pfunz   Wie bitte? (*What are you saying?*)

Gabriel   Ich bin nicht ihr Neffe. (*I'm not her nephew.*)

Von Pfunz   Wer sind Sie dann? (*Then who are you?*)

Jeanne   We discovered this morning that this poor boy –

Gabriel   Vor vier Nächten bin ich an den Strand gespült worden. Lily hat mich gefunden und hierher gebracht. Diese Familie hat mein Leben gerettet. Ich war bewußtlos bis gestern, und als ich aufwachte, hatte ich alle Erinnerung über mich selbst verloren. (*I was washed up on the beach four nights ago. Lily found me. She brought me back here and this family saved my life. I was unconscious until yesterday and I woke remembering absolutely nothing about myself.*)

Von Pfunz   Nicht möglich . . . (*No . . .*)

Jeanne   I do think you might speak in English.

Gabriel   Meine gesamte Erinnerung ist mir völlig entschwunden. Selbst mein eigenes Spiegelbild hat mir angst gemacht. Die Nebel haben sich zwar ein wenig gelüftet; aber trotzdem konnte ich mich gestern nur an ein oder zwei seltsame Bilder erinnern – allerdings nichts über den Krieg. (*I'm suffering from a complete loss of memory. My own image in the mirror made me afraid. The mist has cleared a little; yesterday, I remembered only one or two strange images, and quite remarkably, nothing about the war.*)

Von Pfunz   Was, Sie wußten nicht, daß Krieg ist? (*You didn't know there was a war?*)

Jeanne   What are you telling him, Gabriel, dear?

Gabriel   Stellen Sie sich nur vor! Was auch immer ich für einen Unfall hatte, mein Erinnerungsvermögen muß einen Schock dabei erlitten haben. Als ich herunter kam und Sie traf, hatte ich keine Ahnung wer Sie waren! (*Can you imagine? I can only believe that my mind has been traumatised by whatever accident has befallen me. I came down and met you, and I didn't have a clue who you were!*)

Von Pfunz   Das ist wahr, meine Uniform! (*That's right, my uniform!*)

Jeanne   Gentlemen please, I insist you talk in English!

Gabriel   Today, things are much better. I know all about the war, and I know exactly who you are.

Von Pfunz   Incredible . . .

Jeanne   What has he said?

Von Pfunz   He is a lost man.

Gabriel   I was found naked, carrying no identification, nothing. They just took me in.

Von Pfunz   Who are you, my friend?

Gabriel   There are various theories. Major, it's the most extraordinary thing. When you have no past, you can't think of the future so the present becomes everything. I can't tell you how vividly I've lived this last day. When your memory of human contact deserts you, each face you meet is so rich, you long to know each character. My past is one day old. I've got no idea if I'm the same man I was, or if this has shaped me into someone else, completely. There's no reply to your question. I don't know who I am.

Von Pfunz   This is unbelievable . . .

Jeanne   It would be, only we found out who he is this morning.

Von Pfunz   Oh? . . .

Gabriel   (*giggling*) Die denken, daß ich ein übergeschnappter Bankangestellter bin, der auf die Barrikaden gegangen ist . . . (*They think I'm a bank clerk, who's gone on some kind of a rampage . . .*)

Jeanne   Speak in English, please!

Von Pfunz   *What* did you say?

Gabriel   They think I'm a bank clerk who's gone on some kind of rampage.

Von Pfunz   Ha! A bank clerk? Ha!

Lily   (*to Lake*) Did you tell him this?

Lake   It's the truth. His name's John Gilbert.

Jeanne   He went missing from St Peter's Port a few days ago.

Von Pfunz   And does he speak fluent German?

Lake   He works translating for your lot.

Gabriel   Apparently I'm a dying man Major. I've been given a death sentence.

Jeanne   Allow me to explain –

Von Pfunz   Have they threatened you?

Gabriel   (*amused*) No. They tell me I have a *thing* on my brain, a tumour I suppose – the reason I remember nothing. I'm dying.

Von Pfunz   But this is absurd!

Lily   (*to Lake*) How could you? How could you tell him that?

Von Pfunz   This must be a joke! . . .

Jeanne   I'm afraid not.

Lily   (*to Lake*) You think he's a bank clerk? Look at him. He's no more a bank clerk than I am! I quite agree with you, Major, this must be a joke. I've spent more time with him than anyone, and I know.

Jeanne   Lilian –

Lily   It's understandable for Mrs Becquet to say he's this man, because she'll have committed no crime by hiding him –

Jeanne   Keep quiet please.

Lily   But . . . his whole manner, his whole bearing, everything! He's not an island man – he's not a bank clerk! I just don't believe it.

   Pause.

Von Pfunz   Who do you think he is?

Lily   I think he's one of you.

Von Pfunz   Ja?

Lily   Mrs Becquet told us one of your officers was lost at sea. I think it's him. Last night in his sleep he was mumbling in German. It's the language he dreams in.

Gabriel Lily, I was awake all night! Why are you telling him this?

Von Pfunz She's telling me what she thinks I want to hear. But the last thing I want to hear, is her lies.

Lily I'm not lying. You just asked me what I thought!

It becomes clear during the following, that Gabriel is fighting pain. He tries to hide it.

Jeanne I think further speculation as to who he is, is pointless. It'll be easy to have him identified. He's got a wife in St. Peter's Port. We'll postpone our trip and you can take him there right now.

Von Pfunz Forgive me, we were talking about something different.

Jeanne We were talking about John Gilbert.

Von Pfunz No. I was speaking of the canker in your house, of this malignance under your roof. Everything this woman has ever said to me has been a lie.

Lily stands.

Jeanne I won't have you insulting my family.

Von Pfunz Jeanne, you are so close you can't see, but it's clear to me. I see the greater truth . . . She ruins your relationship with your son. She transforms this little girl into something unnatural and puts nails in this young man. Jeanne, it's beneath you to protect her.

Lily He knows . . .

Von Pfunz What do I know, Fraülein?

Lily (*agonised, to Gabriel*) You told him.

Gabriel No.

Jeanne Lily . . . he deceived me.

Von Pfunz You were calling for help.

Jeanne You must be mad! (*To Lily.*) He tricked it out of me, I swear! . . .

Von Pfunz Your spirit was speaking with mine.

Jeanne You have to believe me Lily, I'd never do this! He's been holding it over me for days! . . .

Lily Mrs Becquet . . . he'll *kill* me.

Von Pfunz Nonsense.

Jeanne If you try and take her from here I've got ways of stopping you. I know the entire civilian Controlling Committee and I'm a personal friend of the Bailiff. This won't be allowed!

> *Estelle gets off Von Pfunz's knee. During the following she goes to Gabriel and looks at him.*

Von Pfunz But the Controlling Committee has passed the law saying Jews must be registered. They have washed their hands! . . . Jeanne, I understand your compassion but it is *malign*. You must tear it from your heart. Even the child turns from the Jew, you see? It is the natural thing. (*To Lily.*) I want you to come with me to St Peter's Port this afternoon. There, we shall go to your own police and you must tell them, nice British bobbies, all the correct information. We just want the truth.

Lily He'll kill me!

Estelle (*whispers*) Now Gabriel . . .

Von Pfunz You should be proud of your race. You should state what you are.

Lily I'll end up in that place, Mrs Becquet, my hair in that room full of hair.

Jeanne   Lilian –

Lily   (*to Von Pfunz*) That's the truth, isn't it?
Discarded . . .

Von Pfunz   (*bewildered*) She has read my book . . .

Estelle   (*whispers*) Now.

Gabriel   (*through controlled pain*) I read it to her. Last
night.

Von Pfunz   *Why?*

Gabriel   I thought she ought to hear.

Von Pfunz   That is my private book . . .

Gabriel   This morning, we read a couple of pages to Mrs
Becquet and Mrs Lake. I think it would be fair to say that
they found it obscene.

Von Pfunz   It is *sacrilege* you have done.

Estelle   Smite him.

Von Pfunz   My poems . . . you don't understand –

Gabriel   Yes I do. They have a madman's eloquence.

Von Pfunz   They are *private*!

Gabriel   How can you possibly call them poetry?

Estelle   Do it now! –

Gabriel   They're *diseased*. I'm a child and I can see that.
The purity of darkness is –

   Gabriel cries out. He stumbles into the chalk square.

Gabriel   Estelle! –

Von Pfunz   What happens with him? . . .

Estelle   (*trying to support him*) No, no don't fall! Don't fall! Gabriel! . . .

Gabriel   – Help – me! –

Gabriel goes into a spasm of pain. He tries to escape it.

Estelle   No, no! Gabriel . . .

Lily   (*approaching*) Give him space, Estelle! Let him breathe!

Gabriel passes out and lies still, face downwards. Estelle kneels by him.

Estelle   (*howling with disappointment*) Wake up!

Von Pfunz   (*approaching him*) What is wrong? Why does he do this?

Jeanne   Because he's a lunatic. I tried to tell you and you wouldn't bloody listen!

Von Pfunz   This is not possible. The young man is ill . . .

Lily   It's the result of his fall. Give him space Major, he doesn't need you crowding around.

Von Pfunz   It is you that should give him space. How can he recover with this creature near him? It is this woman who has made him ill!

Von Pfunz virtually pushes Lily out of the way. She retreats.

Von Pfunz   Jeanne, send to The Hermitage for my men. They will get the doctor here. He has been injured . . .

Von Pfunz tries to turn Gabriel over.

Estelle   Leave him where he is!

Von Pfunz Little girl, don't order me around. I have first aid facts.

Von Pfunz turns to Jeanne. Estelle pulls the dagger out of Gabriel's belt.

Von Pfunz Jeanne you do nothing! You stand there like a statue. – Send for my men! I need my men!

Lily (*becoming hysterical*) They'll take me away. They'll take me *away*! Jeanne, you stupid, evil cow. I'll never forgive – never forgive –

Von Pfunz We must save this –

Jeanne Estelle!

Estelle plunges the knife into Von Pfunz's belly. She clings to Gabriel. Von Pfunz stands and staggers. A patch of blood begins to grow on his uniform.

Lake Lord Jesus . . .

Von Pfunz Das Kind, ich bin verwundet . . . (*The child, I'm hurt . . .*)

Jeanne What have you *done*?

Von Pfunz collapses against Jeanne. Estelle starts screaming. The next happens quickly. Many of the lines come over one another.

Von Pfunz Jeanne . . .

Jeanne Margaret, help me!

Lake Put him in that chair.

Lake and Jeanne help Von Pfunz to a chair. He groans.

Von Pfunz I will bleed to death!

Estelle Gabriel . . .

Jeanne   Get something!

Lake searches for clean cloths.

Estelle   I *hate* him! Make him *die!*

Lily   Estelle, it's all right. It's all right.

Estelle   He was going to put you in jail . . .

Estelle sobs. Lily hugs and comforts her.

Estelle   I love you Lily, I love you, I don't want him to take you away . . .

Jeanne   (*to Von Pfunz, fiddling with his clothes*) Sit still! I can't get this damn thing open! Margaret!

Lake   Here.

Lake shoves some cloths at Jeanne.

Jeanne   Get him a drink.

Lake fills a glass of Cognac.

Lily   Give me the knife, Estelle. Come on, you don't need it . . .

Estelle drops the knife.

Jeanne   Lilian, go to The Hermitage and get his men. He needs a doctor.

Lily   No.

Von Pfunz   This bitch would watch me die! . . .

Lake   There's a *child!* Watch your language!

Jeanne   For God's sake – (*Aside, to Lily.*) She's stabbed him in the spleen; he'll bleed to death.

Lily   I won't help him.

Jeanne   You'd see Estelle take the blame?

Estelle   (*shrieking*) No!

Jeanne   Lily, let her go. Get his bloody men!

Estelle   (*clinging to her*) No! He'll put me in *jail!*

Von Pfunz   I swear on my life, I won't put you in jail;
please, Mrs Myles, put down the child; get me help . . .

Estelle   SAVE ME!

Lily   I won't let him near you, Darling, I won't let him
near. It's all right . . .

Jeanne   Margaret, for God's sake go!

Lake   You sure that's what you want?

Jeanne   Do you think I want my child accused of
murder?

Lake heads for the door. Jeanne follows.

Jeanne   Don't tell them who did it! Just say there's been
an accident . . .

Lake   Keep him talking if you want him to live. And keep
that cloth pressed on the blood. Jean, I'm not running.

Lake exits.

Jeanne   I tried to tell you he was mad but you wouldn't
bloody listen. If you'd damn well listened this'd never've
happened! He's a bloody lunatic!

Estelle   Why won't he wake up?

Lily   I'll look after things now. You go to your room.

Estelle   No!

Lily   Now, Estelle. I mean it.

Estelle   He needs me.

Lily   Upstairs!

Estelle   I'm staying with him. He's gathering power.

Lily picks up the knife.

Von Pfunz   Jeanne, this has killed me . . .

Jeanne   It's a bloody scratch, you pathetic fool.

Lily approaches Von Pfunz. Jeanne sees the knife.

Lily   Mrs Becquet.

Jeanne   What are you doing?

Lily   Perhaps it'd be a good idea if Estelle went upstairs.

Jeanne   (*to Estelle*) Get upstairs!

Lily   (*to Von Pfunz*) How many of you know I'm Jewish, Major?

Von Pfunz   I told them all. All of my friends in The Hermitage.

Estelle   That's not true! He hasn't got any friends. The Krauts up there laugh at him behind his back!

Lily   Thank you.

Jeanne   (*to Estelle*) Upstairs, now!

Estelle   Gabriel needs me.

Jeanne goes to Estelle, and bundles her out of the room. Estelle protests.

Jeanne   Upstairs, or I'll give you the biggest thrashing of your life!

Estelle exits. Jeanne holds the door shut. Estelle bangs on it, crying.

Von Pfunz   My God . . . (*He giggles weakly.*) You come to finish me off . . .

Jeanne   Put it down, Lilian; this is ridiculous!

Von Pfunz   Are you going to kill me?

Lily   It's self-defence.

Jeanne   (*to Lily*) Don't you dare! This is *my* house!

Lily   Then you do it!

Lily holds the knife to Von Pfunz's throat. She pulls his hair.

Von Pfunz   There's a moment that will come, if you hold the knife inside me, when my heart will seem to beat with yours. It is passionate, to kill.

Lily makes ready. Von Pfunz whimpers. For a second, she hesitates. Von Pfunz grabs her hand and takes the knife from her.

Von Pfunz   We are not all as brave as a ten-year-old child, ja?

Lily knocks Von Pfunz off his chair. He cries out in pain. She pushes past Jeanne, and bundles the hysterical Estelle upstairs. There is quiet. Jeanne helps Von Pfunz into a sitting position. He leans against her.

Jeanne   I didn't think she'd do it. She won't even throttle the hens. Here. Drink.

Jeanne gives him the Cognac.

Von Pfunz   Look at this knife. A child has killed me . . .

Jeanne   (*taking it from him*) Try to calm yourself, Johann.

Von Pfunz   (*calming*) You do not desert me.

Jeanne   Keep still. Margaret will bring your men.

Von Pfunz   I must say everything to you.

Jeanne   Don't say anything.

Von Pfunz   It is my deepest desire.

Jeanne   I don't want to know.

Von Pfunz   My deepest desire . . . to be loved by you.
Jeanne, I know that is not possible. (*Pause*.) I shall say the
Jew stabbed me.

Jeanne   What?

Von Pfunz   I shall protect your little girl. The Jew shall
take the guilt.

Jeanne   No! (*Pointing to Gabriel*.) Say he did it!

Von Pfunz   I can't do that.

Jeanne   Why not?

Von Pfunz   It would be a lie. The Jew tried to kill me.

Jeanne   He's dying anyway!

Von Pfunz   So is she.

Jeanne   Please do one good thing! One thing!

Von Pfunz   The boy is *innocent* . . . that is good.

Jeanne   Please; if you love me . . . .

Von Pfunz   No. NO! I save the little girl because I love
you! In Poland . . . it is true. I saw things, things that
would . . . I saw the ground move in the thaw, so many
bodies buried underneath. I thought it was hot springs . . .
I was in this place. I saw these children . . . The dead are
all the same Jeanne, all the same. Me, you, all the same.
No salvation. They make fertiliser from the bones. This
room of women's hair, a vault, vast, they turn it into cloth,
sell it for sixteen pfennigs a yard. And I see this. I see it
with my soul . . . So I write my book, I write all these
things and I think, Jeanne, I think what is the greater
truth? (*Crying*.) I do this so the children of the future will
thank me. This creates a pure Europe. I spoil myself for

them. I tread my soul in this mire for them. The cruelty becomes clear. It is like a dream in my mind . . . a pure Europe . . . like light . . .

Jeanne (*pointing to Gabriel*) He stabbed you.

Von Pfunz You don't *listen*!

Jeanne (*desperately*) *He* stabbed you!

Von Pfunz NO!

Jeanne stabs Von Pfunz.

Jeanne Then I have to . . .

Von Pfunz Jeanne!

Jeanne I do listen. And this is what I think.

Von Pfunz dies. Jeanne pulls the knife out of him. Her hands are covered in blood. She shudders. She looks at Von Pfunz. She pulls herself together.

Jeanne Disgusting.

Jeanne goes to Gabriel. She puts the knife in his hand. She smears blood onto his hands and his cricket whites. She goes to the sink and washes her hands. Gabriel comes round.

Gabriel Falling . . .

Jeanne approaches him. She looks at him and gently touches his hair.

Gabriel Mrs Becquet.

Jeanne You poor boy. I'm so sorry . . .

Gabriel I could see a river. Like a flash in my mind. A great river. Sun on it, the noise, everything. It seemed . . . familiar.

Jeanne There aren't any rivers on Guernsey.

*Pause. Gabriel lifts a hand to touch her. He sees the
blood. He becomes aware of the knife. He sits up.
He sees Von Pfunz.*

Jeanne   You went into a frenzy and stabbed him.

Gabriel   No . . .

Jeanne   I saw you do it.

Gabriel   (*pause*) Estelle.

Jeanne   She's been in her room all morning. The Major
tried to arrest you. Surely you remember? . . . You resisted.
It was horrible. You stole my knife and plunged it into
him. Twice. I tried to save his life.

Gabriel   Is that the truth?

Jeanne   Yes.

Gabriel   I don't remember.

Jeanne   Oh, my dear . . .

Gabriel   I'm lost, Mrs Becquet.

Jeanne   I'm so sorry.

Gabriel   (*looks at the corpse*) Dead. So. I killed him.

Jeanne suppresses tears.

Jeanne   When Myles was a little boy, I thought the best
gift I could give him was experience. It had come so
painfully to me and I wanted to spare him. So I taught
him what I knew: the world is full of liars and trust is a
game for fools: those who give, fail; those who take,
succeed – and other such . . . wisdoms. He became experi-
enced. But of course he stopped trusting me. He was right
to. I'm a liar.

Gabriel   Do you really believe he's dead?

Jeanne nods her head.

Gabriel   Your daughter believes in angels.

Jeanne kisses Gabriel. She immediately stands and looks away.

Jeanne   Do you want them to find you here?

Gabriel   No.

Jeanne   Then run. Get out.

Gabriel   Where's Lily?

Jeanne   With Estelle.

Gabriel   Will you tell her –

Jeanne   Of course. Of course I will.

Gabriel stands.

Gabriel   Which way is the sea?

Jeanne   Down the hill. Please run, if you can . . .

He goes to the door.

Gabriel   I don't know who I am.

Jeanne   My dear . . . You're Gabriel Lascalles.

Gabriel   (*slowly nods*) Auf Wiedersehen.

Gabriel leaves.

Jeanne   Forgive me.

Jeanne suddenly cries. Lily appears at the door. She looks at Von Pfunz.

Lily   Who killed him?

Jeanne   Gabriel. He came round, just after you left the room. I couldn't stop him. To tell you the truth, I didn't try.

Lily   Where is he?

Jeanne   Gone. To the beach.

Lily   Who are your tears for, Jeanne?

Jeanne   I'm not crying.

Pause. Lily goes to Von Pfunz. She pulls the book out of his pocket. She holds it.

Lily   I couldn't do it.

Jeanne   Do you feel like a coward?

Lily   Yes.

Jeanne   Don't . . .

Lily   (*pause*) I can't stay here, Jeanne.

Jeanne   Where will you go?

Lily   I don't know.

Jeanne   Then stay.

Lily looks at Jeanne. Neither gives much away. Estelle enters, smiling through her tears.

Estelle   I saw Gabriel, running to the beach. So fast . . . his feet weren't touching the ground. I could tell.

Jeanne is standing near to Estelle. She reaches for her hand.

Discover the brightest and best in fresh theatre writing
with Faber's new StageScripts

Sweetheart by Nick Grosso

'His ear for the youthful argot is acute, his individual
scenes vivid. *Sweetheart* looks good and sounds good.'
Evening Standard

Sweetheart premièred at the Royal Court Theatre, London,
in January 1996 and toured thereafter.

Mules by Winsome Pinnock

'A fascinating, kaleidoscopic look at black female drug
smugglers shuttling between Jamaica and London, buying a
few months of freedom, sometimes ending up in jail, never
meeting the "top people", dreaming of a new life. Pinnock
is always good on exiles in transit, the pull of the homeland.'
Observer

Mules was produced by Clean Break Theatre Company.
The play premièred at the Royal Court Theatre, London,
in April 1996 and toured thereafter.

The Wolves by Michael Punter

'Punter not only writes beautifully and intelligently,
but he plays on the very idea of language. It is an
exceptionally meaty debut.'
Guardian

The Wolves was produced by Paines Plough Theatre
Company. The play premièred at the Bridewell Theatre,
London, in March 1997

All Faber StageScripts are priced at £4.50.
If you cannot find them stocked at your local bookshop
please contact Faber Sales Department on 0171 465 0045